PERSONAL STRUGGLES

Oppression, healing
and liberation

To my parents, Angela and Sean, who consistently modelled the importance of acting with integrity and treating all people with complete respect

PERSONAL STRUGGLES

Oppression, healing and liberation

Dr Seán Ruth

SERIES EDITOR: Dr Marie Murray

ATRIUM

First published in 2019 by Atrium
Atrium is an imprint of Cork University Press
Boole Library
University College Cork
Cork T12 ND89
Ireland

Library of Congress Control Number: 2019949089

Distribution in the USA Longleaf Services, Chapel Hill,
NC, USA.

British Library Cataloguing in Publication Data
A CIP catalogue record for this book is available from the
British Library.

ISBN 9781782053484

Typeset by Studio 10 Design
Printed by Gutenberg Press in Malta

www.corkuniversitypress.com

CONTENTS

MindYourSelf   viii

Foreword   1

Acknowledgements   4

1. Identity, Struggle and Hurt   5

2. How Oppression Hurts Us   21

3. Internalised Oppression and Domination   43

4. Healing the Hurts of Oppression   67

5. The Liberation Process   87

6. Taking Charge of Our Struggles   107

Glossary   128

Other Resources   130

Other Reading   133

Index   137

DR MARIE MURRAY has worked as a clinical psychologist for more than forty years across the entire developmental spectrum. An honours graduate of UCD, from where she also obtained an MSc and PhD, she is a chartered psychologist, registered family therapist and supervisor, a member of both the Irish Council for Psychotherapy and the European Association for Psychotherapy and a former member of the Heads of Psychology Services in Ireland. Key clinical posts have included being Director of Psychology in St Vincent's Psychiatric Hospital, Dublin, and Director of Student Counselling Services in UCD. Marie served on the Medical Council of Ireland (2008–13) and on the Council of the Psychological Society of Ireland (2014–17). She has presented internationally, from the Tavistock and Portman NHS Trust in London, to Peking University, Beijing. She was an *Irish Times* columnist for eight years and has been author, co-author, contributor, and editor to a number of bestselling books, many with accompanying RTÉ radio programmes. Her appointment as Series Editor to the Cork University Press *MindYourSelf* series gathers together a lifetime of professional experience to bring safe clinical information to general and professional readers.

DISCLAIMER

This book has been written for general readers to introduce the topic or to increase their knowledge and understanding of it. It is not intended, or implied, to be a substitute for professional consultation or advice in this, or allied, areas. Any content, text, graphics, images or other information provided in any of the *MindYourSelf* books is for general purposes only.

On topics that have medical, psychological, psychiatric, psychotherapy, nursing, physiotherapy, occupational therapy, educational, vocational, organisational, sociological, legal or any mental health- or physical health-related or other content, *MindYourSelf* books do not replace diagnosis, treatment, or any other appropriate professional consultations and interventions. This also applies to any information or website links contained in the book.

While every effort has been made to ensure the accuracy of the information in the book, it is possible that errors or omissions may occur. Research also leads to new multidisciplinary perspectives in all professional areas, so that, despite all the publishers' caution and care, new thinking on certain topics may alter the accuracy of the content. The authors, editors and publishers can, therefore, assume no responsibility, nor provide any guarantees or warranties, concerning the up-to-date nature of the information provided.

MindYourSelf

Few expressions convey as much care as that lovely phrase 'mind yourself'. Quintessentially Irish, it is a blessing, an injunction, an endearment and a solicitous farewell. Like many simple phrases, 'mind yourself' has layers of psychological meaning, so that while it trips lightly off the tongue at the end of conversations, there are depths of kindness that accompany it.

Being told to 'mind yourself' touches the heart. It resonates with the longing in each of us to have somebody in our world who cares about us. Saying 'mind yourself' means 'you matter to me', what happens to you is important, and may nothing bad befall you. It is a cautionary phrase, with a gentle acknowledgement of your personal responsibility in self-care. Although it has become so ingrained in our leave-taking that we may not consciously note it, unconsciously, being minded is an atavistic need in all of us. 'Mind yourself' is what parents say to children, to adolescents, what people say to each other, to family and friends. We also say it to reassure ourselves that we have reminded those we love to keep themselves safe.

It is in this spirit of recognising the importance of self-care that the *MindYourSelf* book series has been designed; to bring safe, researched, peer-reviewed information from front-line professionals to help people to mind themselves. While, at one level, information – about everything – is now on multiple platforms at the touch of a screen, relying on internet sites is a problem. What is true? Who can you trust? How do you sift through the data to find what you need to know? Because it is not lack of access to facts, but fact overload, that makes people increasingly conscious of the dangers of misinformation, contradictory perspectives, internet prognoses, and the risk of unreliable or exploitative sources. What people want is simply the information that is relevant to them, delivered by professionals who care about their specialities and who are keen to help readers understand the topic. May this Cork University Press *MindYourSelf* series find its way to all who need it, and give readers the tools and resources to really mind themselves.

Dr Marie Murray, Series Editor, *MindYourSelf*

FOREWORD

There are some books that need to be written and read. *Personal Struggles: Oppression, healing and liberation* by Seán Ruth is one of them. It invites us to recognise social injustices, inequality of opportunity, unequal power, pervasive prejudice, and to open our eyes to the pain of discrimination – however unintentional – that we may inflict on other people. It gives detailed description of how the experience of oppression affects feelings, behaviour and relationships and the ways in which people blame themselves for their personal struggles, and for problems for which they are not responsible. With compassion and care, Seán explains why people see their problems as personal failures instead of recognising the failure of society to value, respect and support them appropriately. This applies particularly to certain groups of people who are oppressed, marginalised, cast aside or stereotyped. 'People struggle,' he writes, 'not because there is something fundamentally wrong with them, but because they face, or have faced, real difficulties in their lives.' He describes those difficulties in detail: how they hurt, how they can be healed, and how individuals and groups can empower and liberate themselves from negative identities that have been foisted upon them.

The book adopts an approach to psychological health that focuses on the social origins of problems rather than on genetic, medical, biological, psychopathological or individual factors. This makes it particularly relevant for service providers in the areas of sociology, education, psychology, psychotherapy, health, social work, and youth and community work. It is a guide for members of marginalised groups who want to develop their own leadership skills. It also provides personal insight for people from privileged situations so that they may see through the eyes of those who are less advantaged.

In content and style, Seán writes in his own fluid, understated way, building up ideas, questions, exercises and activities to help readers deal with their feelings and heal their hurts. Section by section, page by page, chapter by chapter, the reader is guided – carefully, methodically and incrementally – through the text. New information is dropped in lightly, core ideas are repeated and reviewed, so that the reader 'learns' ways of countering and resisting the consequences of oppression, such as anxiety, poor self-esteem, or a lack of voice, validity, legitimacy and power.

Seán also addresses the paradox of mental colonisation, by which those who are oppressed often absorb and internalise the views of the oppressor, to the extent that they can inadvertently collude in their domination. The longing to belong can make people deny themselves, their rights, and their difference, as they try to mimic the behaviour of oppressors in order to be accepted and included. Recognising this, the book invites people who are marginalised to resist it, to reclaim their sovereignty by challenging that oppressor voice in themselves and in others. It also asks those who think they are benign and free of prejudice to take another look at themselves.

While Seán's work clearly derives from solid theoretical foundations and research (writers such as Fanon, Freire, Foucault and Boakye come to mind, in addition to social psychologists such as Harré, Mead, Smail, Shotter and Gergen), he does not distract the reader with academic treatises and pedagogical references. Instead, he reaches a general audience with a practical, easy-to-follow discourse, based on his decades of experience as an organisational psychologist working internationally in leadership development, conflict resolution and diversity. Evident too is his attention to what are called the 'Social GGRRAAACCEEESSS', an ever-expanding acronym for gender, geography, race, religion, age, ability, appearance, class, culture, ethnicity, employment, education, sexuality, sexual orientation and spirituality that was developed between systemic therapists John Burnham, Alison Roper-Hall and colleagues since the 1990s to help identify the grounds on which many people are discriminated against.

This is a book that goes beyond traditional psychological analysis. The sensitive manner in which it is written belies its strong political message. But the message is clear. We live in a society that is unfair. And if this book is a plea for healthy psychological development, for throwing off the shackles of domination, in whatever form they take, it is also a book that challenges each of us to take action, to recognise how extremes of power or powerlessness can lead to violence and despair. It tells us, whether we like it or not, that we all belong to dominating groups. Even by default, we can be blind to our privilege, our power and the possibilities open to us that are not available to other people.

We can all identify people who are outcasts in society today. We are aware of discriminatory practices, social injustices, negative ascriptions, gender inequalities and false representations that can influence how we understand people and how we behave towards them. So while we may have societal regrets about those who were ill-treated in the past, we continue to subjugate and reject others, replacing former victims with new candidates. Seán Ruth reminds us, most powerfully, of the need for constant vigilance in how we treat each other and the world in which we live.

Dr Marie Murray, Series Editor, *MindYourSelf*

ACKNOWLEDGEMENTS

I am grateful for the support of many individuals during the preparation of this volume. In particular, I want to thank Marie Murray, *MindYourSelf* Series Editor, who provided valuable advice and encouragement at all stages in the process.

I would also like to thank all at Cork University Press, especially Mike Collins, Publications Director; Maria O'Donovan, Editor; Aonghus Meaney; and Alison Burns.

Many other people played a part in the development of this work. I am indebted to Pamela Uhlemann, who was stalwart in her feedback and belief in the project. I have learned so much from my children, Aoife, Diarmaid and Conall. Their thinking and their example continue to inspire and teach me. Finally, the many people I have worked with and who have attended my workshops over the years played an important part in deepening and clarifying my understanding of personal struggles and how we can deal with them. Thank you all.

CHAPTER 1

Identity, Struggle and Hurt

INTRODUCTION

Have you ever wondered why some people face so many struggles in their lives? Have you wondered why you yourself find life a struggle sometimes or why particular situations are hard to handle? Do you ever find yourself overcome with intense feelings of anger or fear or sadness without understanding what has triggered these? Making sense of these difficulties is at the heart of this book.

Traditionally, psychology has tried to explain these things in terms of the individual. So, people are seen to face difficulties because of their personality, for example. Or perhaps because they have a neurosis or mental health problem of some kind. Or maybe it's to do with their genetic makeup, and so on. The problem is seen to be the person and the solution is to do something with that person.

In this book, we take a radically different approach. We think about people as social beings. This means that their behaviour cannot be fully understood separately from what's happening around them in their family, their community or in the wider society. People struggle not because there is something fundamentally wrong with them but because they face or have faced real difficulties in their lives.

While there may be many positive aspects to our lives or our relationships, it is also the case that our experiences in family, community or society can be a source of great pain and hurt. For many of us, these experiences may include violence, abuse, inequality, destructive relationships, or differences in how we are treated by the wider society. If we truly wish to understand our own or other people's behaviour, we need to know how these processes operate and how they affect people individually and collectively. And if we want to make our own or other people's lives better, instead of blaming the individual we have to do something about what causes difficulties in the society around us.

STRUGGLE

In thinking about all of this, one useful concept to begin with is *struggle*. If we look at those around us, for example, particularly as we get to know them, it is safe to say that everyone experiences life as a challenge, at least part of the time. There is no one who does not struggle to one degree or another or at one time or another. Some people's struggles may be tougher than others at times, but no one escapes.

Even though we have this in common with everyone around us, we often give ourselves a hard time. We act as though we were the source of these difficulties and as though only 'weak' people struggle. We tell ourselves that we shouldn't have these recurring problems or that a 'better' or 'stronger' person would have overcome them. We feel guilty, ashamed, inferior, bad, inadequate or some other negative emotion in the face of how we struggle. Such feelings are understandable but not accurate or justified.

There are reasons why we struggle that have to do with the kind of world we live in and for which we are not to blame. This is why the word *struggle* is a useful one. It describes what we do or what we face, not what we are. It also avoids the negative connotations associated with alternative terms such as 'weaknesses' or 'shortcomings' that imply that personal inadequacy is the source of our problems. Understanding the social origins of our distress and how they affect us is one of the purposes of this book.

SOCIAL IDENTITY

Another concept that is most useful is *social identity*. Humans are complex, yet we tend to think of ourselves as a single being with a particular identity that we sum up as our 'personality'. We see ourselves or others as outgoing, or shy, or friendly, or cynical, or aggressive, and so on. None of these descriptions capture fully who we are, however. In reality, we are a collection of many different social identities, each with particular strengths and particular struggles. We can think of our gender, our class, our sexual orientation, our religion, our nationality, our skin colour, our age, and many other possible ways of defining ourselves.

Each of these identities has a life story attached to it. This life story describes the positive experiences we have had and the strengths we have developed as well as the hurts we have experienced and the struggles we have endured. An interesting thing to do is to tell our life story as a female, or as a male, or as a person with a disability, or as a gay person, and so on. When we think about how we got hurt, it wasn't just because of the person we were. Many of our hurts were because of a particular identity we had or that other people attached to us. If we didn't have that identity, we probably would not have experienced those hurts. We tend to think of our hurts as personal to us as individuals. However, as we tell our stories and as we hear other people's stories, we begin to see that there is much more to it than that. There are patterns to these stories that people have in common, and as we notice these we can move from blaming ourselves for our struggles to seeing how, in a sense, we have been set up to struggle.

Salient Identities

Not all our identities carry the same weight. The significant or salient identities – those that have most played a role in shaping who we now are (loosely speaking, our personality) as well as those that have an impact on our current relationships – vary from person to person. For some people, the identity that explains or makes most sense of their life experiences is their gender. What happened to them as females or as males had a huge impact on how they now feel about themselves or on their relationships or on the choices they made in life. For others it is their sexual orientation. Growing up and living in a society that was hugely homophobic placed severe limits on the kinds of relationships they could have and on how they could express or show themselves. And, again, for others it is their class background. Class determined the options available and how people could feel about themselves. For many people, it is a combination of such identities, with each one having an influence on how they see themselves, their relationships or the world around them. Part of knowing who we really are is being able to name these salient identities and the influence they have had on us, for good or ill, over the course of our lives. Naming them is not a once-off activity but an ongoing part of our growth and development as people.

In general, because of the structure of our society, there are particular identities that are primary or salient for most people and other identities that are more specific to particular individuals. Gender and class, for example, tend to have a significant impact throughout society. Being adopted as a child, on the other hand, is salient for a much smaller number of people, but for those within that group it may have very deep effects. In this sense, from the point of view of society, all identities are important even if some of them affect a smaller number of people. The challenge for each of us is to pinpoint the specific identities that have shaped our own lives.

Pinpointing our identities is something we can really only do for ourselves. Other people cannot usefully dictate from the outside what our most significant or salient identities are. One of the difficulties people experience is that others sometimes attach particular identities (or labels) to them and then proceed to make assumptions about them or mistreat them on the basis of prejudices or stereotypes that they associate with those identities. At the same time, people may also miss or ignore some of a person's significant identities and unknowingly say or do things that hurt and add further to their struggles.

In the end, becoming aware of and naming our salient identities is a journey of self-discovery. This is a work in progress for each of us and some of what we judge to be our important identities may change over time as our circumstances and our relationships change. As we claim these significant identities, we will find that our lives are enriched and that we gain not just a better understanding of ourselves but also a greater sense of power over who we are.

Oppressed and Oppressor Identities

The examples of race, gender, sexual orientation and class illustrate an important aspect of identity. Within some of our identities we experience inequality and mistreatment and within others we experience power and privilege, along with the possibility of hurting or abusing others. In this way, our various identities are typically a mix of what we call oppressed and oppressor roles. So, for example, a white, working-class, gay man or a black, upper-class, heterosexual woman have a mix of these oppressed/oppressor roles.

At workshops, I often ask people to make a list of all the oppressed groups they can think of. (We use lots of different terms to describe such groups, including disadvantaged, underprivileged, minority, marginalised, subordinate, and so on.) This invariably turns out to be a long list, and it quickly becomes apparent that everyone present is a member of at least one of these oppressed groups. In fact, if we think about it, each of us can claim membership of a number of oppressed groups. Belonging to some of these groups has had a big impact on our lives. Whether we realise it or not, these particular identities have played an especially significant role in our lives both positively and negatively. Being able to name them can help make sense of the struggles we face.

In the same way, when I ask groups to make a list of all the oppressor (or dominant, elite or privileged) groups they can think of, it again becomes clear that everyone is, at the same time, a member of at least one oppressor group and often of a number of oppressor groups. Many of these also play a significant role in defining who we are in both positive and negative ways. As we shall see, we tend to be much less aware of our oppressor identities than our oppressed identities, but being able to name these can be a very enlightening and empowering experience.

So, it is clear from all this that one person's thinking, feelings and behaviour may be strongly shaped by their oppressed experiences as a young, female person of colour and by their oppressor experiences as a middle-class heterosexual, for example. Another person may be shaped by being working class and gay and, at the same time, being male and white. Once again, the point is that we cannot fully understand our own or anyone else's behaviour without knowing the significant identities and their effects.

Naming and clarifying the impact of our various identities is an ongoing process and one that gives us much greater control over our lives and how we respond to life's challenges. Often, the claiming of an identity changes the way a person thinks about themselves and marks a significant turning point in their life. We often see this, for example, when someone comes out as gay. Or consciously claiming being female can change how a woman sees herself. (One particular example of this was a white person I worked with who was an activist on an anti-racism project and who was shocked to realise that they had never claimed being white, although they were very definite about the other people's identity as black.) As we do this, we see our lives and our struggles as part of a much bigger picture. We move from blaming ourselves and feeling powerless to blaming a system of oppression and then reclaiming power over our lives.

Identity and Feelings

One reaction that people have in trying to name their oppressed or oppressor identities is that they sometimes don't *feel* oppressed or *feel* like an oppressor. However, in naming our various oppressed and oppressor identities, our feelings are not necessarily a good guide. A really effective oppression, for example, will encourage people not to feel or see themselves as oppressed. They will not recognise the extent to which they are oppressed. They will just see things in terms of some personal inadequacy and blame themselves.

In a similar way, people with an oppressor identity will tend to see their power and their privilege as a personal entitlement or part of the natural order of things. Many people with an oppressor identity do not recognise how oppressive they can be. They do not feel oppressive and do not attach great importance to that identity. I sometimes ask groups of men or white people what they like about themselves as men or white people. A common response is that they don't think of themselves in these terms. If I had asked what they liked about themselves *as people*, they would have been much more able to answer the question. The problem is that, although they don't think of themselves in terms of these identities, women or people of colour who interact with them will be unlikely to lose sight of the fact that they are male or white. Unless people are aware of behaving in obviously oppressive ways, they will tend to see themselves as relatively benign and free of prejudice and to underestimate the significance of their oppressor identity.

In practice, it is often easier for us to name our oppressed identities. The nature of the mistreatment we suffer and our day-to-day struggles make it hard to ignore the reality of our oppression. On the other hand, trying to name our oppressor identities can bring up confusion, resistance or denial, particularly when we don't feel that we are oppressive or if we don't see ourselves behaving in obviously abusive ways. The sad fact is that many of us are unaware of the ways in which we think or behave oppressively and this is one of the great difficulties in relationships between people with different identities.

We can get a more accurate picture by looking objectively at what happens in society to the particular groups to which we belong, rather than looking at how we feel. While I may not personally feel oppressed, it can be seen that people like me, as a group, are systematically mistreated. Or, while I may not feel oppressive, it can be seen that people like me, as a group, hold power and privilege and that people from my group are the source of the mistreatment of others. The issue is not whether or not I *feel* oppressed or oppressive but whether or not I belong to groups to which these experiences often apply. Regardless of how I feel, acknowledging my oppressed and oppressor identities can make a huge difference to my self-image and to my relationships.

What this also means is that claiming an oppressed or, especially, an oppressor identity does not mean that I am claiming to be a bad person. Claiming an identity is not about people being good or bad, it's simply a statement about the social groups we belong to and what happens to them in our society. We shall see more clearly as we go on how, regardless of our identities, our underlying goodness remains intact.

Claiming Our Identity

So how do we go about naming and claiming our identities? At the heart of this process are the simple acts of telling our story and hearing other people's stories. Sometimes, as we listen to other people talk about their lives, we realise that their stories resonate with us. We notice that we have had similar experiences or we share similar feelings. We find ourselves thinking, *So I'm not the only one who had those feelings* or *Oh, so that happened to you too*. As we tell our own story, we notice similar reactions from our listeners. In the end, we realise that it's not just me!

As we see a similarity in each person's story, we begin to name the identity we have in common. We realise that these patterns were common to us as women, or as Catholics, or as Muslims, or as Jews, or as people of colour, or as people who are poor, or as children of people with alcohol addictions, or as Travellers, and so on. We can see that it wasn't by accident or chance that these things happened to us. They tended to happen to anyone with our particular identity.

Claiming our various identities is a starting point on a journey towards healing our hurts and reclaiming our power. Later we will encounter other steps in the process. But it begins with our realising that we don't struggle because there is something wrong with us. We struggle because bad things have happened to us and they happened to us because of our identity.

People sometimes object to this focus on our identities. They question why we need to attach labels to people and argue that we should just see everyone as human beings. Thinking in terms of identities or using labels to define ourselves is seen as divisive. This is an understandable reaction but it misses an important point. The reason we claim an identity is because we got hurt and conditioned under that identity. We can't free ourselves from that identity until we heal the hurts or undo the conditioning that went with it. And we can't do that unless we first claim the identity. At the end of that process we will be free to discard the identity if we wish, but it doesn't work to bypass the step of claiming it in the first place. Over and above this, however, it turns out that claiming our identities is often a liberating and a unifying experience rather than a divisive one. The following chapters will explore this in more detail.

INHERENT CHARACTERISTICS

The value of claiming our identities becomes clearer if we understand something very important about human nature. Our behaviour and our personalities are a reflection of our experiences within our social identities. At the same time, it is also the case that there are particular characteristics that are true of all people inherently or by their very nature as human beings. These characteristics are universal (they apply to everyone) and they are permanent (we never lose them). Let us imagine a perfect scenario where a new human being comes into the world not having experienced any trauma in the course of their mother's pregnancy and having a natural, trouble-free birth in the presence of a group of adults who were relaxed, undistracted and excited to welcome this new person into their lives. What could we expect about this new human?

People born in such ideal circumstances would probably experience the following:

• They would feel closely connected to the people around them.

• Their relationships would be characterised by feeling loved and being loving.

• Their ability to think clearly and flexibly about the world around them would be unimpaired.

• Their ability to learn would be substantial.

• Their experience of life would be joyful and exciting.

• In the absence of emotional and physical trauma, such new human beings would have access to the full range of human ability and to close, loving, cooperative relationships with those around them.

• They would not be held back or limited by doubts about themselves or their ability, by painful feelings of fear, hatred, anger, worthlessness, shame, and so on.

• They would have all the personal resources they needed to cope with the challenges and struggles they might encounter in the course of their lives.

Of course, this is an ideal picture. In reality, this is not what we experience. What we see are people who struggle in relationships, who have doubts about their own worth or their goodness, who feel overwhelmed by the challenges facing them or struggle to come up with workable ways of dealing with life's difficulties. The relevance of the ideal picture, however, is that it tells us that we do not come into existence with these shortcomings as part of our inherent nature. We acquire them as a result of what we experience rather than being pre-programmed to be inadequate.

It is neither accurate nor useful to believe that some people come into the world blessed with positive attributes and others arrive condemned to inadequacy or inferiority. By nature, all humans are inherently loving and lovable, inherently good, intelligent, powerful, creative, spontaneous, playful, and all of the other positive qualities we see expressed across the human population. These qualities are universal. They are true of everyone.

The only reason we don't see this clearly in practice in ourselves or others is because of the experience of emotional and physical hurt or trauma. So, although in a real sense these positive qualities are permanent, we can be disconnected from or lose access to them. If we hadn't been hurt, we would not have lost our connection to our intelligence, or our power, or our spontaneity, or our creativity, or the many other human qualities that are part of everyone's inheritance. In practice, people experience damage, hurt or trauma either before, during or after birth and in the course of their lives. Depending on the extent of the hurt and how that hurt is dealt with, we can lose our access to, or the ability to use, the natural, inherent qualities that are part of our humanity.

As we shall see, these hurts can be healed and our connection to our inherent human qualities can be restored. Because they are permanent, these human qualities are still part of us and true of us inherently despite any hurts. We can think of our hurts as sitting on top of these qualities and blocking us from them rather than not

16

having these qualities in us at all. This is a hugely important way to think about ourselves, with lots of valuable implications that will be explored in the coming chapters.

While this way of thinking may seem to rest on a number of assumptions about human beings and their basic nature, they are valid assumptions to make. They may be difficult to prove conclusively but they are consistent with so much of what we know about people and their lives. They are consistent with what we know and experience about very young people. They are consistent with the accounts that adults give of their upbringing and consistent with what we learn from the collective experiences of oppressed groups as they describe what happens to them in society. The perspective on people adopted here turns out to be a very useful and workable one in practice and ongoing experience seems to confirm its underlying assumptions. There is a principle that says, when faced with competing possible perspectives, always choose the one with the most interesting possibilities. Although we can't prove beyond doubt that this is an accurate picture of human beings, adopting it opens up a rich and empowering set of options for each of us.

HURT AND RECOVERY

Hurt can happen in a number of different ways. Sometimes it happens purely by accident. Someone gets into difficulty while swimming and nearly drowns. Afterwards, they are afraid of the water and lose their enjoyment of swimming. No one is to blame. It was accidental.

A second way that hurt can happen is through contagion. In this case, someone else who has been hurt passes on that hurt to people around them. So, for example, someone who grew up being heavily criticised is now highly critical of others. Or someone who was beaten as a child has now gone on to beat their own children.

A third source of hurt is the operation of oppression. In this case, there is a system of mistreatment that installs hurt on people with particular identities. So, we get hurt because of sexism or racism or some other 'ism'. Much of what we will talk about here is related to this third source.

In global terms, the least important source of hurt is accidents. This is not meant to diminish the impact of accidents when they occur. They can have huge effects on individuals and groups, and much of what follows is equally relevant to this source of hurt. In terms of the scale of hurt, however, in terms of its overall impact on groups within society, accidents are not the main source of the damage that occurs. Instead, contagion and oppression account for most of the hurt we struggle with.

The good news is that we can recover from hurt and get back our connection to our humanity, to our inherent human characteristics. An important part of that recovery process is understanding the ways that oppression damages us, individually and collectively, and what we can do, individually and collectively, to liberate ourselves from it. How this recovery process works will be explored in the coming chapters.

CONCLUSION

By nature, all of us are completely good people. But we have acquired hurts through accident, through contagion and, most importantly, through oppression that have left us struggling. These struggles are not a sign that there is something wrong with us inherently. Instead, they are rooted in what is happening in the society around us.

Each of us is also a collection of different social identities, some oppressed and some oppressor. These identities have shaped how we think, how we act and how we feel. Understanding how they have affected us is central to taking charge of our lives.

Ultimately, we can recover from the hurts we have suffered, we can undo the effects of oppression and we can liberate ourselves and others.

Questions

1. How have you experienced oppression in your life?

2. How did these experiences leave you feeling about yourself or the world around you?

3. In spite of these experiences, what aspects of your inherent humanity have you been able to stay connected to (for example, your sense of worth, your courage, your goodness, your power, your intelligence, and so on)?

CHAPTER 2

How Oppression Hurts Us

We saw in the previous chapter that one of the effects of our experience of hurt is that it cuts us off from a connection to our inherent, positive human qualities. We lose a sense of what's special and good about ourselves. This hurt is not random or accidental. Most of it happens to us because of the identities we have, for example as working-class people, or as women, or as men, or because of our sexual orientation, or any of a large number of other identities. In this chapter, we want to look more closely at how this process works and what effects it has on us.

We can sometimes see this more clearly from the outside. When you work or live with people who share the same social identity (for example, as women or as working-class people or as Travellers or as gay people, and so on), over time you get to notice the ways in which the difficulties and challenges they face can take a heavy toll on them, both individually and collectively. As you spend time with them and listen to their stories, you begin to see patterns or themes in what they describe or experience. You notice that people face many of the same struggles or they express similar feelings about the situations facing them. Sometimes you can see this reflected in particular ways that people think, sound, look or act. This common experience that people share can be thought about and understood in terms of oppression.

WHAT OPPRESSION DOES TO US

To begin with, think of different groups that stand out because of the way they are treated within society. There are various ways we can describe such groups. For example, we can think about groups around which there is a lot of prejudice or stereotyping. People from these groups are seen as inferior, or dangerous, or uncivilised, or stupid, or dirty, or worthless, and so on.

Perhaps we might not use as strong a word as prejudice to describe how these groups are viewed. Maybe it is just that they are not held in as high regard as other groups. Their needs are not as important as those of others, for example. Or maybe it is simply that we feel awkward or ill at ease around them; we don't know how to act in their company or how to talk to them or be with them. Perhaps groups such as these are simply ones that people make assumptions about that are not based on any factual evidence or deep understanding. People who are not members of these groups make pronouncements about what they are like or what is good for them, what they need, how they should behave, or how they ought to be controlled. As we saw in the last chapter, we use a variety of terms to describe such groups – oppressed, disadvantaged, underprivileged, marginalised, subordinate, minority, and so on.

We also saw that if we make a list of all the groups that would possibly match these descriptions, it quickly becomes clear that everyone is a member of at least one, and probably more, of these oppressed groups. We all experience oppression within one identity or another, and much of where we struggle in life is directly related to these experiences of oppression. This raises a number of questions:

- Do we know what oppressed groups we belong to?

- Can we say what effects these oppressions have had on us?

- How have they affected our confidence or our self-esteem?

- What effects have they had on our relationships with people who share the same identity as us?

- What effects have they had on people with a different identity?

- What have they done to our sense of power in our lives or our ability to take leadership?

- In an overall sense, do we know how they have affected how we feel, how we think or how we act?

23

Before reading any further, see if you can make a list of some of the oppressed identities that you carry. You could base this list on the ways you feel oppressed in your life. You could also base it more objectively on whether or not you belong to groups that you know are treated negatively or less favourably than others in society.

Having identified some oppressed groups you belong to, keep these in mind as we look at how this process plays itself out. Given the negative attitudes, assumptions or feelings we have described here, what happens next? We can see the process outlined in Figure 1.

Mistreatment

When we think of particular oppressed groups, the first thing to notice is that the various prejudices, stereotypes or assumptions that people carry about these groups don't just stay in people's heads as private or hidden attitudes, thoughts or ideas. They get acted out in various forms of mistreatment. People find themselves on the receiving end of physical or verbal abuse, discrimination, unequal treatment, disrespect, exclusion, and a whole range of other reactions.

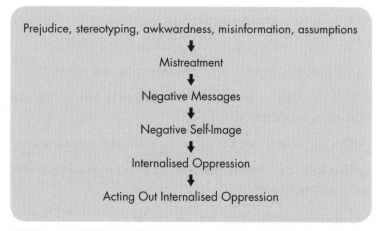

FIGURE 1: THE PROCESS OF OPPRESSION

This mistreatment is quite systematic in the sense that it is not random or accidental. It is built into how society works and is perpetrated through the education system, the legal system, religion, the mass media, the workplace, and so on. When it is part of the system like this, the mistreatment is better described as oppression. And because it is systematic, it is never just a one-off occurrence. It is experienced repeatedly in one form or another by people in the oppressed group.

Overt vs. Subtle Oppression

The different forms of oppression range from very obvious, overt reactions to very subtle, hard-to-pinpoint, negative reactions. We can see examples of these in the box below (Figure 2). At the overt end, when we experience oppression, we are in no doubt about what has happened and who is responsible for it. We have just been beaten or verbally abused, for example. The oppression is easy to name.

OVERT		SUBTLE
Violence	Exclusion	Rigid niceness
Discrimination	Offensive jokes	Insensitive language
Verbal abuse	Arrogance	Low expectations
Harassment		Condescending

FIGURE 2: VARIETIES OF OPPRESSION

As the oppression becomes less overt, however, we may find it harder to identify. We may find ourselves being excluded socially but we're not sure if this is accidental or deliberate. Or we may have to listen to jokes or comments that are offensive to, or demeaning of, people like us. It's not clear if these are deliberately meant to make us feel bad or if it would be okay for us to object to them. We might feel like we are making mountains out of molehills if we say anything in reply or if we're not absolutely certain that what happened was actually oppressive. This discomfort adds to our uncertainty, our distress and our self-blame – we question the reality of our emotions, the intentions of other people, and our own capacity to distinguish what is deliberately oppressive and what is not.

At the very subtle end of things, we may find that we cannot easily put our finger on what has happened but we know we feel bad about something. We can't point to anything specific but we just don't feel at ease or safe around particular people. Or, for some reason, we feel bad about ourselves when in their company. Sometimes other people seem to treat us well but it is actually their unnatural niceness that makes us feel uncomfortable. Or we notice that, even though they seem to treat us well, they have very low expectations of people like us. Perhaps they use language that is meant to be inoffensive but it is not the language we ourselves use. For example, settled people may refer to Travellers as 'itinerants' or men may refer to adult women as 'girls'. Or maybe we pick up a tone in what people are saying that we experience as a put-down or a criticism. The words don't seem critical but there is an underlying judgement, arrogance, condescension or superiority that we react to. At this end of the scale, what has happened is so subtle that we end up feeling bad, but confused about why we feel that way.

Much of the oppression that we experience comes in these subtle forms. They have sometimes been described as micro-assaults. We find it difficult to name them or interpret them and the other person may or may not be aware of the effect they are having. Even people who see themselves as our allies might have difficulty spotting what's happening since it is so subtle.

If we are a member of one of the groups described above, there is no way we will escape the experience of oppression. The actual form of the oppression or the degree of it may vary from person to person, but no one fully escapes it. At a very minimum, we see it happening to the people around us and, from the stories people tell, it is clear that witnessing mistreatment can be almost as damaging as directly experiencing it.

Negative Messages

Every time we experience mistreatment or witness the mistreatment of people who share our identity, we get a set of negative messages about ourselves. We hear that we are in some way inferior. We hear that we are less significant or worthwhile than other people. We hear that our views are not as important or worth listening to as other people's views. We hear that our needs are not as much a priority as other people's needs. We hear that in lots of different ways we are second-class citizens.

These negative messages are picked up on two levels. I hear that there is something wrong with me personally. I am worthless, stupid, inferior or second-class. But I also pick up these messages about all of my people, those who share the same identity as me. So not only do I hear that I am inferior, I also hear that anyone who shares my identity is inferior. We are all second-class.

Negative Self-Image

Because of the repeated and systematic nature of oppression, the negative messages come at us frequently and from many directions. We hear these messages repeatedly and in numerous ways, sometimes throughout our lives. We experience them in one-to-one interactions, in the mass media, at work, in church, at school, on the streets, in the courts, and in various other situations. Over time, the repetition of these messages has an effect on our self-image. If I am told often enough that I am second-class, I will eventually begin to feel and to think of myself as second-class. If I hear often enough that I don't count or that I'm less intelligent than other people, I will eventually feel and think of myself as unimportant or stupid. Repetition is an insidious way of convincing me of my second-class status.

This effect on our self-image can be seen on two levels: I will come to think of myself personally as inferior or insignificant and I will come to think of all my people as inferior or insignificant. In this way, the whole group comes to see itself as inferior or insignificant. It becomes hard for me personally and for us, as a group, to feel good about our identity.

This wider, collective effect on the group is often obscured, however. If everyone around me feels bad about themselves, then feeling bad seems normal. If I grow up in an environment where no one feels significant, then feeling insignificant seems natural. It doesn't look like there is anything going on to cause these bad feelings; it just looks natural. If people feel inferior, it must be because they are inferior. If I feel bad, it must be because there is something wrong with me and not that there is something wrong with the system that sets people up to feel this way.

Internalised Oppression

By the end of this process, what had started out as an external oppression has become internalised. What began as someone else's prejudice or stereotyping or misinformation is now internalised and 'believed' by members of the oppressed group. At this stage, the hurt that started from the outside has been adopted within the group. We start to pass on the negative messages to each other. It only requires an occasional reinforcement from the outside to maintain the negative messages and the poor self-image. It is clear that if people didn't internalise the oppression, they would simply refuse to put up with it and would take active steps to end it. At this stage, however, people from the oppressed group come to accept, 'agree with', or 'agree to' their inferior or victim status. One of the things that people don't fully realise is that most of the damage done by oppression happens when we internalise it.

I sometimes use the example of a woman and her young daughter who called to my house one morning. When I opened the door, she said, *I'm not a Traveller but I'm married to one*. This was all she said but you can imagine the unspoken piece – *So don't slam the door in my face* or, *Treat me with some respect*. This woman had learned to accommodate the oppression by slightly distancing herself from being a Traveller in the hope of being treated better. But think of it from the point of view of the little one beside her who hears her mother say this at every door. Think of the messages this little one gets about her own identity. 'Why does my mother keep saying this?' 'What's wrong with being a Traveller?' Even if I treat her mother with complete respect, her daughter still gets the negative messages. At this point, the oppression has been internalised and is now being passed on within her own family.

Acting Out Internalised Oppression

Once the oppression has been internalised, we start to act out the negative messages and feelings that are part and parcel of it. So if I am told often enough that I am inferior, after a while I will start to feel and think of myself as inferior and will begin to act accordingly. The acting out of internalised oppression can take many forms. We may go silent in certain situations, become self-critical, become invisible when we are in mixed groups, or become apologetic or ashamed. We may act in ways that communicate that we don't expect to be treated well, or give up making demands or having expectations of other people, or we may settle for a second-class status. Occasionally, some of us become defiant and oppositional, but despite appearances, this is still coming from within the internalised oppression. We shall explore these effects further in the next chapter.

HOW IS OPPRESSION DEFINED?

So far, I haven't actually defined precisely what I mean by oppression. This account of how oppression affects us allows us to make a clear distinction between simple mistreatment and oppression. Mistreatment is a random, purely personal occurrence that happens to people as individuals and not because of their particular social identity.

Oppression, on the other hand, can be thought of as *the systematic, one-way mistreatment of the members of one group by those of another group that has become institutionalised and is defended*. It is systematic in that it is built into the system and is not accidental or random. It is one-way insofar as it goes from a high-power group to a low-power group rather than the other way around or being a two-way process. In the case of men and women, for example, we can say that men oppress women but it is not accurate to say that women oppress men. Men may be mistreated by women but the oppression systematically goes in the other direction. In the same way, we sometimes hear people remark that women oppress each other. By this definition, however, women may mistreat one another but the oppression always comes from the outside. This distinction is important. People from an oppressed group do not oppress each other. As we shall see, they may act out their internalised oppression and mistreat each other but that is a different process from oppressing each other. Even though, in practice, mistreatment may sometimes hurt just as much as oppression, it helps to be precise about the terminology we use here in order to be clear about how this process works.

Given the systematic and therefore predictable nature of oppression, once we know someone has a particular oppressed identity, and even though we know very little about that particular person, we already know a lot about what they are likely to experience in life. The oppression targets everyone with that identity, and although the detailed effects will vary to some degree from individual to individual, the broad pattern of their experience can be guessed at. As we saw, the oppression is built into the system and no one with the oppressed identity escapes it completely.

LEVELS OF OPPRESSION

Another way of looking at this process is to think in terms of different levels or layers of oppression. Imagine a situation where one group wants to dominate another one. There are various ways in which it can try to do this, different mechanisms it can use to achieve its goal. These are illustrated in Figure 3.

PHYSICAL OPPRESSION
Violence, rape, genocide, imprisonment, segregation

ECONOMIC OPPRESSION
Poverty, unemployment, low pay, austerity, debt, zero-hour contracts, poor/dangerous working conditions

PSYCHOLOGICAL OPPRESSION
Mental health labels, academic justifications for inequality, stereotyping, incitement of fear/hatred, propaganda, control of media

INTERNALISED OPPRESSION
Belief in our own inferiority and powerlessness to change anything

FIGURE 3: LEVELS OF OPPRESSION

Physical Oppression

One obvious way to try to dominate another group is physically. The oppressor group can use violence ranging from beatings right through to murder. Rape and sexual abuse is also a common tool of domination. In the case of indigenous peoples and Jewish people, for example, the experience of genocide is at the heart of their oppression. People from the oppressed group can also be imprisoned and kept separate or segregated, both in relation to education and where they live. For physical oppression to work, it isn't necessary to attack every individual member of a group. If enough people from the group are targeted, the remainder can be scared into submission.

The problem with physical oppression from an oppressor's point of view is that, although it can be hugely damaging to people individually and collectively, it's not an 'efficient' means of maintaining control. Additionally, it is more visible than other oppressive forms. People are in little doubt that it is wrong, it can give rise to resistance, and it can require a lot of resources to police the oppressed group.

Economic Oppression

The effectiveness of oppression can be increased if it is reinforced with economic oppression. In this case, members of the oppressed group are faced with poverty, low pay, unemployment, debt, zero-hour contracts, temporary work, austerity measures, and so on. The demands of day-to-day survival mean they do not have the time or the energy to try to change things. By keeping them preoccupied with economic survival, they are less likely to organise to resist the oppression.

Psychological Oppression

The impact of the oppression can be increased further if we add a layer of psychological oppression. Here, for example, the second-class status of the oppressed group is reinforced and justified by 'experts' from the mental health system who medicalise the oppression by attaching labels that define people as mentally ill, or by academics of various kinds who defend and legitimise the inequalities as either natural and/or inevitable. The expert stance legitimises the perception of inadequacies in the oppressed groups, sending subtle messages that their inferiority is either endemic or self-inflicted. This is added to by the mass media or by politicians, who blame and stigmatise particular groups for what is wrong in society, who incite fear of, or resentment towards, particular groups or who reinforce and spread negative stereotypes of groups. Essentially, what happens here is that the dominant groups and institutions make pronouncements from the outside on what is wrong with oppressed groups and why the unequal treatment they receive is necessary, justifiable or unchangeable.

A significant part of this third layer is what has been called mental health oppression. This encourages people to see themselves as the problem rather than some external system. Their feelings and struggles are attributed to their own inadequacy. This is often facilitated by theories of mental health that fail to acknowledge the impact of oppression in people's lives and that advocate treating people through medication or therapies that view struggles as exclusively personal or as biological or 'genetic'. Some psychotherapeutic approaches, for example, may see attempts to frame problems in terms of sexism or racism or some other oppression as evidence that clients are not taking sufficient responsibility for themselves. In this way, despite the efforts and good intentions of many of those involved, the mental health system can become part of the system of oppression. This is further supported by a profit-driven pharmaceutical industry that has a vested interest in medicalising people's struggles and producing drugs to control or numb their feelings.

Internalised Oppression

The combination of these first three layers of oppression is very powerful in keeping any individual or group oppressed. The final layer has the effect of locking in the oppression. It does this by ensuring that the oppression becomes internalised, as we saw earlier. Now people see themselves as the problem. These four layers of oppression make it very difficult for groups and individuals to clarify or name what is happening and to organise against the oppression. We can see how each of these layers comes into play in relation to specific groups, and part of what is called 'consciousness raising' involves detailing the ways this happens.

CULTURAL COMPETENCY

A different way of thinking about the process of oppression is in terms of stages of cultural competency. This focuses on what happens in the relationship between a dominant, oppressor group and the oppressed group. We can also think of it in terms of what happens between individuals from these groups. It is possible to describe this relationship at different stages of development:

- Stage 1: Cultural Destructiveness

- Stage 2: Cultural Incapacity

- Stage 3: Cultural Blindness

- Stage 4: Cultural Pre-competence

- Stage 5: Basic Cultural Competence

- Stage 6: Cultural Proficiency

At Stage 1, *Cultural Destructiveness*, the relationship is characterised by attitudes, policies and practices that are destructive of the oppressed group and its culture. Attempts are made by the dominant or oppressor group to eliminate or destroy the oppressed group or its culture, which are seen as inherently inferior or a threat. Genocide, ethnic cleansing, suppression of native languages, religion or spirituality, and theft of native lands have characterised the experience of many oppressed groups, particularly indigenous peoples, at this stage. In recent years, we have heard a lot more about how children were removed from their families and sent for adoption or raised in institutions that tried to suppress their language, religion and culture.

At Stage 2, *Cultural Incapacity*, the system or its agencies do not intentionally seek to be culturally or physically destructive, but they remain extremely biased, believing in the superiority of the dominant group and assuming a paternalistic posture. There is a lot of ignorance, stereotyping and fear of the oppressed group, who are tolerated so long as they accept their inferior status. There is bias and discrimination against, and low expectations of, the oppressed groups and lots of messages, both subtle and not-so-subtle, that they are fit only for menial, second-class roles. Often, the groups will be kept segregated in one way or another in order to maintain their differences.

At Stage 3, *Cultural Blindness*, there is an expressed philosophy of being unbiased, a denial of any differences between the cultures and a pretence at equality. However, everything is judged in terms of the values and experiences of the dominant culture. The oppressor group operates on the assumption that they are unbiased, that everyone is the same, that skin colour, gender, ethnicity or culture make no difference to how people are treated, and that the helping approaches used by the dominant group can be universally applied to all groups without the need to take account of language, cultural or other differences. There is a tendency to ignore or be unaware of the strengths of the oppressed group, to blame the victims and to judge people by how closely, or not, they resemble members of the oppressor group. At this stage, it has become difficult to deny the existence of an oppression in the past but there is a pretence that things have changed and that everyone is now treated the same.

With Stage 4, *Cultural Pre-competence*, there are the beginnings of real awareness within the oppressor group and some acknowledgement of weaknesses in the ways they operate. There is a stated com-mitment to equality and a desire to get it right in at least some ways. Agencies hire minority staff, explore how to reach out to oppressed groups, initiate training for their workers on cultural sensitivity, enter into needs assessments concerning minority communities, and recruit minority individuals for their boards of directors or advisory committees. In spite of this, there is a tendency towards complacency and tokenism. There may be a simplistic belief that undertaking one initiative or experiment is enough to meet their obligations towards the oppressed group. For example, small numbers from the oppressed group may be employed in non-traditional roles. However, their token status along with their training and the messages they get about what is expected of them may mean they are not much more progressive than members of the oppressor group. People will be hired who are unlikely to challenge or 'rock the boat' or who feel grateful to the oppressor group for the opportunity. If nothing else, their small numbers mean they have limited impact on the system. Although at this stage there is an awareness of the oppression, this is understood mostly in an intellectual way and, in particular, members of the oppressor group have difficulty seeing how their own personal behaviour and relationships are infused with oppressiveness. We can see this in the case of sexism, where, on the one hand, men claim to believe in equality for women and, on the other hand, sexually abuse or mistreat individual women in their relationships or fail to challenge this behaviour when it is apparent among male family members or friends.

At Stage 5, *Basic Cultural Competence*, there is a much greater level of awareness and the beginnings of real change. There is some clarity within the oppressor group about their own prejudices and mental blocks and a commitment to dealing with these as part of their own process of development. Diversity is valued. There is also a commitment to the liberation of the oppressed group and the building of close bonds of friendship and support. This involves a lot more listening on the part of the oppressor group and a willingness to learn from, and be guided by, the oppressed group. There is now a level of humility on the part of the oppressor group and a recognition that the real experts on the relationship are the members of the oppressed group. At the same time, prejudices and unawareness continue to exist and get in the way of true equality.

Finally, at Stage 6, *Cultural Proficiency* (or Advanced Cultural Competence), old feelings of prejudice or arrogance have been discharged and new attitudes and feelings of equality and acceptance have been internalised. The identity of the oppressor group is no longer based on feelings of superiority or dominance over the oppressed group and there is a recognition that they are part of the problem and not just of the solution. There is a willingness to give up control and the arrogant belief that they know best.

It has to be said, unfortunately, that we have very few examples of true cultural proficiency between groups. Occasionally, individuals may reach this level of development, but we still have a long way to go to achieve this at a group or societal level. Using the model of Cultural Competency allows us to assess what type of relationship exists between different groups or between individuals with an oppressed and an oppressor identity and gives us some pointers to the kinds of steps that need to be taken to build a truly equal relationship.

One of the things that the concept of cultural competency highlights is that overcoming oppression requires that the oppressor group grows and develops in awareness in order for change to happen. Within the oppression, the struggles of the oppressed are seen as being due to their own inferiority or inadequacy. Change is seen to involve getting them to change themselves. The alternative perspective holds that *both* groups have to change. This was captured very well in a quotation attributed to Lilla Watson, an indigenous Australian poet, artist and activist, who said:

> If you have come to help me, you are wasting your time. But if you have come because your liberation is bound up with mine, then let us work together.

A NOTE ABOUT CLASS OPPRESSION

Over time, certain oppressions have become widely recognised and they are regularly discussed, if not always clearly understood. We come across many references to sexism or racism, for example, and while people may disagree over whether a particular attitude or behaviour is sexist or racist, few dispute that these oppressions exist. These have become part of the way people make sense of the world around them.

There are other oppressions that haven't achieved that level of recognition and their validity as a means of explaining what we see around us is much more likely to be questioned. One particular example is class oppression, or classism. Although we often see references to people's class background, for example as working or middle class, the notion of class oppression is one that many people are uncomfortable with. In one way, this is strange given that class oppression is actually quite pervasive. The gross inequality between 'haves' and 'have nots' is just one obvious example of this. When we explore it, however, it is clear that classism has had a much greater and much deeper effect than many people realise. Working-class people and people who are poor experience it every day in many different ways, some obvious and some subtle. It is so pervasive that for some it just seems normal and something they learn to live with. Middle-class people are also deeply influenced by their class background but are often unable to name the ways it has affected how they see the world, their sense of entitlement, and the kind of lives they lead. It all just looks normal and natural rather than being a reflection of a system of oppression.

Part of the reason why classism is so rarely discussed is that the people who influence the agenda of what is discussable tend to come from a privileged class and do not experience the oppression as acutely as others. Middle-class academics, for example, who may be quite aware of issues around sexism or racism, often struggle to understand how class operates as an oppression or the forms the oppression takes within any given class or within interpersonal relationships between people of different classes. In fact, many of the struggles we see people having are directly related to their class identity but rarely attributed to that source. One of the challenges we face is to become as aware of how classism operates as we are about sexism or racism.

BEING ALLIES

For those who want to be allies with an oppressed group and bring about change, including people from the various helping or caring professions, a key part of the work entails identifying the patterns of domination and superiority that we have internalised and then freeing ourselves from them. This includes looking honestly at the prejudices we hold and at the situations in which our own feelings cause us to struggle in our relationship with people from the oppressed group. It also means tackling those situations in which we ourselves have been oppressed and where we share similar struggles to those of the oppressed groups.

Some groups have experimented with what are called 'poverty insertion programmes', in which people from privileged backgrounds are sent to live, for a few weeks, among those who are poor. They are provided with similar accommodation and the same income in order to learn about what it means to live in poverty. Often, people have come away from these experiences having learned a huge amount about poverty and the oppression of people who are poor. The interesting thing, however, is that they tended not to have learned much about themselves and what it means to have privilege. The focus tended to be almost entirely on the oppressed group rather than themselves and, in a way, this in itself becomes oppressive. A common problem with attempts to be allies with oppressed groups is the failure to focus on the psychological baggage carried by the allies themselves as a result of their privileged status or upbringing. These and other aspects will be explored in more detail in the next chapter.

CONCLUSION

Oppression is the systematic mistreatment of the members of one group by the members of another group or by society as a whole. One of its major effects is that we internalise various negative messages about ourselves and our people that then shape our self-image and how we think, act and feel. A lot of oppression happens subtly and most of the damage is done when it becomes internalised. While we don't question the existence of many oppressions, the oppression of classism is notable because it is quite pervasive and yet rarely discussed, probably because those with influence often come from a privileged class background.

A question that sometimes arises for people is where oppression comes from. If people are inherently good, as I suggested in Chapter 1, how come they end up oppressing others? Part of the answer to this, as we saw earlier, is that they had already experienced hurt through accident and contagion before there was any oppression. Oppression came later and built on the already-existing hurts that had been acquired. It was not always part of human society and arose historically at particular periods. The first oppressive societies were generally slave societies. Before that, people were able to hurt one another but this was not organised into a systematic mistreatment of one group by another. This systematic mistreatment developed once it became possible to have a surplus of food, when animals were domesticated and food could be stored for later use rather than having to use it right away. At that point, it was possible for one person to produce food for more than just themselves and this allowed for the development of an elite group that did not have to work. Instead of either killing enemies or adopting them into the tribe, they could now be enslaved and put to work to support this elite.

Questions

1. What are the main oppressed groups to which you belong (for example, women, men, working class, LGBTQ+, disabled, people of colour, and so on)?

2. How have you experienced hurt or mistreatment as a member of these groups?

3. What are the main oppressor groups to which you belong (for example, men, middle class, white, heterosexual, and so on)?

4. What privileges or advantages are attached to these identities?

CHAPTER 3

Internalised Oppression and Domination

At the core of most of our struggles is the experience of oppression in one form or another. This may have happened at an earlier stage of our life or it may be happening in the present or it may have been significant throughout our life. One way or the other, it has left us damaged physically, intellectually, spiritually or emotionally or in all of these ways. It has left us feeling bad about ourselves, undermined our confidence and our power, interfered with our having close, loving relationships, and left us confused about the reality of the world around us.

Our difficulties in these areas are not because there is something inherently wrong with us even though we may blame ourselves or others may blame us. The difficulties are largely the effects of oppression and how we internalised that oppression.

It is extremely important that we understand this process. So much of the society around us tries to communicate that there is something wrong with us because of the struggles we face. In reality, there is nothing wrong with us as people. Our struggles are the result of the oppressions we have experienced.

This is not to excuse or justify any mistreatment of others, but rather an attempt to explain why this happens. We have a responsibility to try to change any destructive or irrational behaviours, but, importantly, we are not to blame for these. The fact is that we have always done the best we could under the circumstances, given the hurts we endured and the places where we struggled. If people knew what we have had to deal with throughout our life, the only rational response would be admiration for how hard we had tried. They may disagree with or actively dislike the way we behave, but if they knew what it took to get us where we are, they could only admire how well we have done under the circumstances. It is very important that we distinguish between what we are like inherently as people and the ways we have been hurt and damaged by what we have experienced in life. Inherently, our goodness remains intact no matter how we have been mistreated or how we have ended up as a result.

To fully appreciate this distinction, it helps if we can understand the various ways that oppression becomes internalised and then acted out.

EXAMPLES

Internalised oppression shows itself in many ways. Examples include:

• We feel insignificant, stupid, second-class, ashamed, unattractive, or in some other way inadequate. We experience this as a personal failing rather than something we acquired from outside as a result of mistreatment.

• We try not to stand out or we try to change how we look, speak or act so as to fit in and not seem different.

• We do not value our health and do things that are bad for us. Not having great pride in ourselves or our people, we do not prioritise taking care of ourselves.

• We expect little of, or for, ourselves or our people. Never having received much praise or affirmation, we come to assume our achievements will be limited.

• We assume that our lives cannot be changed and that there is no point in trying to change anything.

• We use alcohol, drugs or other addictions to numb our painful feelings. We turn to any substance or activity that will distract us and ease the pain we struggle with.

• At an individual, family or social level, we find ways to use the system for our own survival or benefit, even at the expense of others in our community.

CHARACTERISTICS OF INTERNALISED OPPRESSION

From these examples, we can identify some common aspects of internalised oppression. While the details may vary from group to group depending on the nature of the oppression, the broad process remains the same across all oppressed groups. In particular, we can highlight seven common characteristics (see Figure 4).

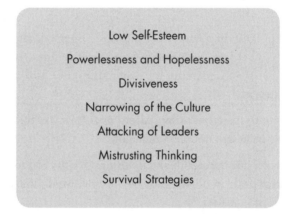

Low Self-Esteem

Powerlessness and Hopelessness

Divisiveness

Narrowing of the Culture

Attacking of Leaders

Mistrusting Thinking

Survival Strategies

FIGURE 4: CHARACTERISTICS OF INTERNALISED OPPRESSION

Low Self-Esteem

All oppressed groups internalise that there is something wrong or lacking in them. We will feel this as individuals about ourselves personally and about our people in general. The specific things we feel bad about depend on the nature of our particular oppression and the messages we receive. For example, feeling stupid or less intelligent than others is a common characteristic of many oppressed groups. Feeling worthless, insignificant or ashamed are other common characteristics.

As we saw before, if we grow up in an environment where the people around us feel bad about themselves, then feeling bad looks normal. The situation offers no contradiction to the stereotype and there is little encouragement for people to feel good about themselves. As with all of these characteristics of internalised oppression, from inside the group these features can look quite normal and are often taken for granted.

Powerlessness and Hopelessness

We internalise that we are powerless to change anything or to resist the oppression. In response to repeated setbacks and defeats, oppressed groups come to believe that there is nothing they can do. This sometimes comes into the open when someone tries to organise for change. People react by pointing out all the ways they are powerless to change things. On the heels of this expression of powerlessness comes hopelessness. People will argue that it is pointless to try anything, that they have already tried and failed, and that further efforts are a waste of time and energy. This will be reflected in the things people say, the way they look and the way they sound.

A relatively common example of this is where a group of people sit around complaining about what is wrong with their group, or their community, or their organisation. It usually begins when someone says something like, *I'll tell you what's wrong with this place.* They then go on to itemise all the things they see as problems. At the end, they give their solution and this often involves getting rid of particular people they blame for the situation. Their contribution is then picked up by the next person, who adds what they think is wrong and who they think is to blame. These contributions tend to be contagious so that other people get pulled into the discussion, which then becomes a long litany of everything that is wrong.

Although on the surface it may look like an analysis of the problems facing a group, in reality it is just a group of people complaining about a situation without focusing on workable ways forward. The effect of such conversations is to leave people feeling drained and to reinforce their sense of powerlessness and hopelessness.

Part of what confuses us here is that in different situations people actually do face some degree of powerlessness. Objectively, they may lack adequate resources or power or support. However, the effect of internalised oppression is to add an additional layer of emotional powerlessness and hopelessness that makes the obstacles seem much bigger than they actually are. It closes down the possibility of positive action.

Divisiveness

A common feature of oppressed groups is the difficulty they face in coming together as a united entity and backing or supporting each other. Instead, they tend to break into factions that compete with and distrust one another. This phenomenon was summed up by the Irish playwright Brendan Behan when he commented that the first item on the agenda is the split!

At a community level, for example, this is reflected in committees or groups that cannot function effectively because of distrust or infighting among the members. Or it may be that people from one part of the community will not support or work with people from another part of the community. While this may appear to be the result of personality clashes, it is rarely as simple as that. Often there is a history or a pattern of divisiveness regardless of the personalities involved.

It is much more useful to view divisiveness first and foremost as a characteristic of internalised oppression rather than personality. If we changed the people involved, we would find that their replacements hit up against the same problems. So rather than being a problem between particular individuals, it is actually due to a pattern of divisiveness that is internalised in the community as a result of oppression.

I saw this pattern with a particular group of women I once worked with. On different occasions, divisions arose between married women and single women, young women and older women, and working-class and middle-class women. Sometimes it was resentment over the amount of attention that was being given to the issues of one group as opposed to another. Other times it was disagreements over whether someone could rightfully claim a particular class identity. Their ability to unite as women was undermined by these other divisions that would surface periodically and cause them to split.

In some cases, divisions are reinforced by outside forces. For example, religious or racial differences may be stirred up as a way of discouraging workers from coming together to fight for better pay or conditions. Or they may be used to prevent people from agitating for political change. We have seen this in recent years in the targeting of groups such as immigrants, refugees or Muslims. But even without this outside influence, the internalised oppression will tend to deter people from supporting each other.

Narrowing of the Culture

Sometimes divisiveness is reflected in a reluctance to accept people as part of the group who do not fit some rigid stereotype. In a lighthearted way we sometimes talk about people being 'blow-ins' to a community. Often, however, there is a heavier degree of exclusion involved. So people may be rejected because they have the wrong skin colour, or the wrong religion, or the wrong nationality, or the wrong accent, and so on. They are rejected even though, in other ways, they share important characteristics of the wider group and face the same struggles.

I once spoke with a woman who identified as French-Algerian.

She said the French would not accept her as French because she was born in Algeria and the Algerians would not accept her as Algerian because her parents were French. She felt she did not know where she belonged as a result.

Often, the narrowing of culture is a reflection of people's negative feelings towards themselves, as they have not yet been able to connect these feelings to a wider process of oppression. As groups reclaim more of their pride and their power, they often become more relaxed about who they will accept as one of their own. At this point, anyone who shares some significant element of the identity will be permitted to claim all the identity. For example, the child of a white mother and black father whose skin colour would allow them to pass as white will be welcomed as a person of colour where previously they might have been excluded or treated with suspicion.

Attacking of Leaders

With many oppressed groups, there is a history of failing to support, or even attacking, their own leaders. Anyone who sticks their head up and becomes visible in a leadership role risks criticism, distrust and isolation within their own group.

There are many examples in Irish history of leaders being attacked by their own people. Similarly, Martin Luther King found that one of the most difficult things to come to terms with was the suspicion and distrust that he was met with from within the black community. While he expected to be attacked by the white establishment, he felt undermined when this was done by his own people.

A working-class woman who was a community activist once described to me the dilemma she faced as a leader. She said that the more visible she became as a leader, the more her friends pulled back from her. The more effective she became, the fewer friends she had and the more she was criticised by those around her.

This process can also be observed within women's groups. A stereotype of women is that they are 'bitchy'. However, so-called bitchiness is actually a characteristic of oppressed groups and not specifically of women. In Australia and New Zealand, they use the 'tall poppy syndrome' to describe how people who stand out are attacked. In Ireland, we talk about 'begrudgery'. These characteristics are not a natural feature either of women or of people from these countries. They are an effect of oppression.

Mistrusting Thinking

Linked to low self-esteem is the tendency for oppressed groups to undervalue or distrust their own thinking or that of members of their own group. We sometimes hear that a prophet is not recognised in their own land. People often comment on how something that is said by an outsider is considered to be much wiser or more intelligent than when expressed by one of their own group. One effect of this is that people may stay silent or not assert themselves in the presence of those from perceived high-status or dominant groups.

An example of this was the board of directors of a community organisation that was comprised of a small group of local working-class people and a much larger group of middle-class professionals. For much of the time, the local people tended to stay silent, defer to the thinking of the professional outsiders, and allow them to set the agenda. But when they became aware of this dynamic and decided to speak up at meetings, they quickly realised that they were much more knowledgeable about the issues facing the community than the professionals from outside.

Survival Strategies

People develop a range of ways to deal with and survive the effects of the oppression. These survival strategies help us cope with the oppression but generally do little to change it. The following are some examples of this:

• We may adopt self-destructive behaviour or addictions to help numb the feelings we struggle with, for example alcohol or drug abuse, gambling or other addictive behaviours.

• We may become defiant in the face of the oppression, reacting aggressively but not in ways that lead to any fundamental change.

• We may become manipulative, learning how to work the system for our own personal benefit or the benefit of our immediate family but not challenging the injustice of the oppression.

• We may turn to criminality or racketeering, even if these take a toll on our own people.

Often, these survival strategies become identified with particular groups. So, for example, alcohol abuse is seen as typical among Irish people, Travellers, or various indigenous peoples such as Native Americans or Aboriginal Australians.

For many groups, part of surviving in a culture involves learning how to assimilate. People take on the language, the religion, the dress, the food and other features of the dominant culture. They change how they look or how they sound. They try to fit in and not stand out as different. While this may enable them to feel safer and more secure, it comes at the price of cutting themselves off to one degree or another from their own culture and their people. In some ways, though, this is more than just a survival strategy. It may be a condition of acceptance into the dominant culture that they assimilate as much as possible and this becomes part of the oppression they experience. We can see this in the reaction to immigrants in particular countries where they attract extremely negative treatment if they speak their own language or wear their traditional clothing.

One particular survival strategy is to find another group of people that we can feel superior to and oppress. Society tends to offer people two choices: we can, at some level, 'agree' to be victims and accept our oppressed circumstances and status, or we can switch roles and become an oppressor to another group in order to feel better about ourselves. (Of course, there is a third option which is rarely held out, and that is to join with others to eliminate our oppression.) This is not to suggest that taking on an oppressor role is a deliberate, conscious decision. It's simply that society may encourage us in various ways to seek relief in this way rather than put our energy into changing society.

This illustrates how different oppressions are interlinked: one oppression holds another oppression in place. For example, a man is oppressed in his workplace. He can get some relief from being a victim by oppressing the women in his life. The women can get some relief by oppressing some other group, such as children or people of a different class, and so on. You would think that, having been oppressed, people from an oppressed group would have a natural empathy for other oppressed people. To some extent that is the case but it also happens that, under certain circumstances, people from an oppressed group can become highly oppressive. So, for example, Irish people who escaped oppression in Ireland by emigrating would later participate in the oppression of black people in the US.

Part of the reason that internalised oppression is so damaging is that it comes to be seen as a natural, inherent feature of people and groups, rather than as an effect of being oppressed. People with an oppressed identity are seen as inherently or naturally inferior. It is as though their inadequacy were built into their genes rather than being the result of a social process that systematically installs doubts about themselves and their people and causes difficulties in the relationships between them.

An aid worker who spent forty years in a developing country once told me that in his view all the people in that country were just lazy. This actually tells us more about him than about the locals. He made the common mistake of confusing the effects of oppression with what is true of people inherently, by nature.

INTERNALISED DOMINATION

While some groups experience oppression and internalise that oppression, other groups experience varying degrees of power and privilege and they internalise patterns of domination. As we saw in Chapter 1, individuals may, at the same time, be part of oppressed and oppressor groups. Within one identity they are oppressed and within another identity they act as oppressors.

Oppressor groups occupy a more powerful or privileged position in society. Just as oppressed groups come to see the internalised oppression as normal and natural, so these oppressor groups see their dominant role as natural and deserved. Among other things, they may internalise that:

- They are entitled to privilege.
- They are superior to other groups.
- Their needs are more important.
- Their thinking is more valuable.
- Their leadership is more worthwhile.
- Their status and material privileges are well-earned and deserved.

They may or may not be conscious of these assumptions, and how they act them out may range from obvious and overt to subtle and indirect. In fact, many people with an oppressor identity tend to be largely unaware of the ways their oppressive attitudes and behaviour show themselves.

Five Mechanisms

We saw earlier that taking on an oppressor role can become part of the survival strategy for people who are oppressed in other ways. Oppressive systems have evolved various mechanisms to induce people to take on this role. If we take the example of class, we can see how middle-class people are set up and encouraged to act in an oppressor role in relation to working-class people or people who are poor. In essence, their role is to help the class system function smoothly and efficiently. We can see similar processes in the case of men. Variations on these mechanisms can also be seen to operate in other oppressive relationships, such as racism, colonialism or religious oppression, for example.

Bribes

Members of oppressor groups are offered incentives, or what are effectively bribes, to help maintain the established order and take on an oppressive role in relation to other groups. This, of course, is not an explicit bargain but the incentives essentially function as bribes that reward people for taking on roles that help maintain the oppressive system. Common examples of these 'incentives' in the case of middle-class people are higher pay and status, greater security, better working conditions, greater material comfort, opportunities to 'climb the ladder', and greater control and decision-making power. In a similar way, men are offered incentives to take on an oppressive role in relation to women. They are given more power, higher status, greater privileges, higher pay, and so on. And this is the case with all oppressor groups where the role confers advantages and privileges that are not available to the oppressed group. The extent to which the disparities have become apparent in media, in the arts, in academic life, in health services and generally in the workplace has confirmed what women always 'knew' – that they were treated unequally and unfairly. This is not to imply that people are conscious of taking on oppressive roles but the rewards induce them to fulfil these functions and not question their impact on oppressed groups.

Threats

Threats go hand in hand with bribes. Middle-class people, for example, fear that unless they conform and co-operate with the system, they will lose their privileges and status, be excluded from middle-class social and professional circles, and end up in the working class. Threats of unemployment, poverty or homelessness add to their fears. The fear of being seen as mentally ill if they do not conform to expectations and go after the privileges on offer may be an additional factor. For people who have not been raised in that class, getting into the middle class and doing well in it is conditional on agreeing to fit in and not to question or challenge the status quo. In a similar way, there is a heavy conditioning of men to fear ridicule, violence, exclusion or other sanctions if they do not conform to the male stereotype. I remember one man many years ago, the father of a young infant, being confronted by men from his housing estate when he took the infant for a walk in a pram. The men surrounded him and told him very directly, *We don't do that here*. The threat of being targeted by gay oppression or homophobia is another influence that forces men into a rigid and narrow male identity. It has been said that oppressive systems are particularly threatened by members of their own oppressor group failing to conform and will employ heavy sanctions to ensure they stick to their expected roles. In addition, in various ways, each oppressor group is set up to be scared of the oppressed group and what might happen if oppressed people refuse to accept their unequal status.

The combined effect of bribes and threats leaves many middle-class people and many men constantly monitoring what they say and do. They also monitor how other people are reacting to them in order to judge whether or not they are acceptable or meeting expectations successfully. In this way, their spontaneity gets suppressed, they learn not to show themselves as they truly are and they become artificial and superficial as a result.

For oppressor groups, in general, part of the price they pay for their privileges is the disconnection from important parts of their humanity. In different ways, people have to be dehumanised in order to hurt other people. If they were allowed to stay connected to their feelings and their humanity, and if they could stay connected to others as people, they would find it very hard to act in oppressive ways. This can sometimes be seen in the relationships between doctors or nurses and their patients, for example. This sense of disconnection is one of the things that makes it hard for oppressed people to be around people from oppressor groups.

Separation

Keeping groups separate is another important strategy that allows people to take on oppressor roles. People who are brought up middle class, for example, are often systematically cut off from poor and working-class people from childhood. Many of them live in different neighbourhoods, go to different schools, and are discouraged from having close working-class friends. If people are brought up working class or poor, or if they belong to a group targeted by another oppression such as racism, a condition of acceptance into the middle class is often to agree to distance themselves from their own people, to one degree or another.

At certain ages, boys are encouraged not to play with or associate with girls. At an older age, they are encouraged to associate with females but only in very rigid, sexualised ways. In Ireland, this was often reinforced by single-gender schools, separate boys' and girls' clubs, and limited opportunities for males and females to connect as people outside their gender identities. Within both genders, individuals are encouraged to compete with one another in ways that maintain and reinforce their isolation.

We can see this same type of separation in other oppressor groups where people may have little or no human contact with anyone from the oppressed group. White people, for example, may never have close human contact or friendship with people who are targeted by racism. Heterosexuals may have very limited connections with people who identify as LGBTQ+, and settled people may have very few friends who are Travellers.

Misinformation

Misinformation about oppressed groups and oppressive systems is another means of inducing people to become oppressors. From earliest childhood, people who are brought up middle class are trained, in crude or subtle ways, to see themselves as more intelligent, important and entitled. They are taught to have low expectations of working-class people or people who are poor and even to fear them. Their separation makes it hard to see the difference between the stereotype of working-class people and what they are actually like inherently.

Whatever their background, everyone is exposed to versions of the same misinformation about the class system and how it works. In this way, inequality is presented as normal, inevitable, or even desirable. People of privilege are exposed to silence about global inequality and the possibility of a fair and just alternative. Mainstream economics, for example, has very little to say about alternatives to the current economic system.

In the case of men and women, people are presented with very limited stereotypes of what it means to be male or female. Men are presented as stronger, more intelligent, more competent, more rational, and as better leaders. Women are presented as weaker, less intelligent, less rational, more emotional, less capable, and as poorer leaders. This misinformation is reinforced in the media, in movies, in religious institutions, in the workplace and other parts of society. The stereotype suggested that to be rational meant being unemotional, which was seen as a male characteristic. It failed to realise that true rationality requires being in touch with feelings, which women are often better at.

Every oppressor group operates with high levels of misinformation and various myths about the oppressed group and few opportunities to discover the inaccuracy of the picture they receive about the oppressed group.

Denial of Reality

In addition to these other mechanisms, there is also a generalised denial of the reality of what's happening in the world. Many young people, for example, wonder why there are those who are treated differently or unfairly. At the same time, the adults around them act as though there is nothing wrong. The inequalities or injustices that they see are ignored or rarely acknowledged. Their perceptions are discounted. Those raised middle class are repeatedly given the message, *Everything is fine*, as though the world is perfectly rational. This is confusing and sometimes frightening and leads many young people to try to conform.

Middle-class adults are surrounded by the denial of class oppression and the distortion of what poor or working-class people face. For instance, cuts to benefits and services are presented as 'reforms' that will improve the system. Some people have been so effectively separated from the majority of the population that they accept this denial, while those who were brought up working class or poor, and who are now in middle-class roles, may feel they have to keep silent about what they understand.

This applies also to gender. The oppression of women is constantly denied or minimised. The myth of equality is held out and many women are encouraged to believe that women's oppression is largely a thing of the past or only true in other societies. Even when the widespread sexual exploitation of women is exposed, for example by the #metoo movement, this is presented primarily as the actions of particular bad men who become reviled rather than as part of a system of sexism and male domination that affects everyone.

HUMANITY

In the face of mechanisms such as these, patterns of domination are upheld and reinforced and people are discouraged from questioning the status quo. However, just as the patterns of internalised oppression are not natural to or an inherent feature of oppressed groups, so also the patterns of domination are not natural to or an inherent feature of oppressor groups.

Taking on an oppressor role does not mean people are bad. Human beings are not oppressive by nature. No one is born sexist, racist or classist. We have to be trained and conditioned to act like this. Society directs huge resources into ensuring that enough people internalise patterns of domination. Regardless of how we are raised or what other identities we carry, we are encouraged to play these roles even from the time we are born. For example, it is almost impossible to grow up male in most societies and not internalise patterns of sexism and male domination. This has nothing to do with the inherent goodness of males but is simply a reflection of the huge process of conditioning that sets up men to act in these ways. Similarly, it is not possible to grow up white in many societies and not internalise patterns of racism. Again, this has nothing to do with people's inherent goodness but is a reflection of the conditioning to see themselves as superior to people of colour.

As we saw earlier, before people become oppressive, they have to be hurt in various systematic ways to make them take on this behaviour. When people with oppressor identities tell their stories, it is clear that deep hurts underlie their own oppressive behaviour. The stories of people raised wealthy or aristocratic, for example, often detail their isolation from close, human contact as they grew up or the fear of radical change or revolution that was instilled in them. These hurts do not excuse that behaviour but we do get a picture of how their oppressiveness originated. We can see that, although oppressor groups get higher status, power and privilege, they pay a price for this in the damage they suffer personally on a human level.

PATTERNS OF DOMINATION

Patterns of domination take a variety of forms. These vary in detail and intensity from oppression to oppression but the broad elements are similar. The following are some common examples.

- Arrogance and Superiority
- Sense of Entitlement
- Stereotyping and Devaluing
- Monopolising Time, Leadership and Resources
- Mistreatment and Violence

Often, members of oppressor groups are unaware of the extent of these patterns in their attitudes and behaviour. Interestingly, however, members of oppressed groups are highly sensitive to such patterns and tend to have a much more accurate picture of what's going on in the relationship than the person from the oppressor group.

Arrogance and Superiority

As a member of a dominant or oppressor group, I am conditioned to think of myself as superior and to display an arrogant attitude in my dealings with people from the oppressed group. As a man, for example, I am encouraged to think of myself as stronger, more intelligent, more important or more competent than a woman. I may act as though my thinking were more valuable than hers and tend to ignore or trivialise the contributions that she makes. As we saw before, these attitudes and behaviours may range from very overt to very subtle.

Sense of Entitlement

As a member of a dominant or oppressor group, I am encouraged to assume that I am more entitled to privilege, respect, attention or leadership. I will also tend to assume that my needs and preferences are more important than other people's. Often, I will take for granted and not notice the work of others that enables me to enjoy my privileges or live in comfort. Here again, I may or may not be aware of the extent of these feelings of entitlement.

Stereotyping and Devaluing

Coming from a dominant or oppressor background, I will tend to have a stereotyped view of people from an oppressed group and to devalue their worth and contribution. The combination of separation and misinformation, mentioned earlier, will mean I am likely to have a very limited understanding of the true strengths and potential of people from the oppressed group, as well as the struggles that they face. This will lead me to mistreat and disrespect them. I may do this in very obvious ways or in subtle ways.

Monopolising Time, Leadership and Resources

My dominant or oppressor conditioning will lead me to monopolise conversations, to expect to be listened to more, to take up more of the time in the relationship, to assume it is my job to lead and to expect and use up more of the available resources. In relationships, much of the work of maintaining the relationship will be done by the other person, who is in an oppressed role. They will take responsibility for ensuring I do not feel bad about myself and agree not to challenge my oppressive behaviour or the various ways in which I act as more entitled or superior.

Mistreatment and Violence

In certain situations, my dominant or oppressor conditioning will lead me to physically or sexually abuse, or behave violently or aggressively towards, people from the oppressed group. This violence will be justified as legitimate, necessary or even harmless. We see this happen around young people and women, for example, where the classic defence of being 'provoked' to violence is a prime example of this behaviour. The guilt is passed to the victim, for provocation, for enticement, for behaviour that elicited violence, without the perpetrator having to take any responsibility for the blatantly violent oppressive actions the other person was subjected to.

NO AVOIDING PATTERNS OF DOMINATION

One of the difficulties for those of us with an oppressor identity is acknowledging the ways that patterns of domination affect us. For example, people can get into a discussion of whether or not they are racist. In an important sense, this is the wrong question. If I am white and I've been raised in a predominantly white culture, the question is not whether I am racist or not but rather to what degree patterns of racism are reflected in my behaviour and relationships. It is not an either–or issue. So when we hear someone say they are not racist or sexist or homophobic, this misses the point.

If we belong to an oppressor group, there is no avoiding internalising patterns of domination to one degree or another. This does not make us bad people. It simply reflects the culture and the conditioning around us. Within this culture, we can ask how the patterns of domination manifest themselves.

We saw in Chapter 2 how oppression can range from subtle to overt. Just because we do not behave in ways that are overtly oppressive, such as with violence or verbal abuse, this does not mean we are free of oppressive behaviour. Other people may still experience us as oppressive in various subtle ways. Part of the difficulty in tackling oppression is that many of us think of ourselves as behaving benignly while being largely unaware of our internalised domination and the ways in which it expresses itself. What sometimes confuses people is the fact that they do not intend to be oppressive. They judge their behaviour by their intentions. However, a lot of oppression is perpetrated by people who are not trying to be oppressive. It's actually more useful to look at oppressiveness in terms of its effects rather than the intentions. Even though we do not intend to be hurtful, our behaviour may still have that effect and, in the end, that's what matters most.

Because the patterns of domination may operate in subtle ways, it can be difficult for us to identify them in our own behaviour. We may have to be guided by the reactions of members of oppressed groups who are much more attuned to our oppressive tendencies. We will generally learn a lot more by trusting the instincts of oppressed people rather than arguing with them or defending our behaviour. This requires openness and humility on our part and a willingness to listen to what people from the oppressed group are telling us, no matter how hard it is to hear. When it comes to what is oppressive, they are the experts.

CONCLUSION

As we have seen in this chapter, a major consequence of oppression is that we internalise a wide range of negative messages and emotions that leave us feeling bad about ourselves and our group. They also cause us to feel hopeless and powerless and, in various ways, separated from our own people. Oppression also affects us within our oppressor identities. We internalise patterns of domination reflected in feelings of superiority, entitlement and mistreatment of people from oppressed groups. All of these internalised patterns have an impact on the relationships we build within and between oppressed and oppressor groups.

As an individual, I have a mix of oppressed and oppressor identities. My internalised oppression is not who I really am. My patterns of domination are also not who I really am. The challenge for me is to discard all of this internalised baggage, reclaim my power, my intelligence and all the other pieces of my humanity that have been squashed, and reach out to build close, human, respectful connections with the people around me.

For some people, power is at the heart of the oppressed–oppressor relationship, and in one sense this is accurate. One of the ways I have tried to deal with it here is through a discussion of powerlessness. However, a sole focus on power can also obscure the complexity of how oppression operates. It is an important aspect, but not the only one. A preoccupation with power can lead us to think of liberation as being about gaining power or the overthrowing of those in power. This has led many liberation movements astray. They ended up taking power and changing the 'actors' while leaving the system of oppression intact. So the focus here is on this wider system, of which power differences are one aspect. Understanding the effects of internalised oppression and internalised domination and the various ways that oppressed groups are set up against each other gives us a much more detailed and accurate picture of this process.

Questions

1. In relation to an oppressed or oppressor identity that you carry, what do you love, admire or respect about people with this identity, for example their courage, their resilience, their caring for one another, their intelligence? (The answers to this question give you a picture of where this group has been able to stay human in spite of the conditioning.)

2. In relation to this identity, what do you not like, what do you hate, what do you feel ashamed of about people with this identity, for example their hopelessness, their oppressiveness, their violence, their shame? (The answers to this question give you a picture of what has been internalised and how people in this group have been disconnected from their humanity.)

CHAPTER 4

Healing the Hurts of Oppression

As we have seen, many of the ways we experience struggle in our lives are a direct result of being oppressed. Sometimes, however, they are also the result of the damage done to us on a personal and a human level as a member of an *oppressor* group. Just as oppression cuts people off from their inherent human qualities, so also taking on an oppressor role disconnects people from important parts of their humanity.

The earlier in our lives that hurts become established, the deeper their effects can be. Later hurts get attached to and build on earlier hurts. Our hurtful experiences as young children in the family, for example, leave us vulnerable to, and are reinforced by, later experiences of oppression within society. In fact, it has been said that the oppression of young people is the training ground for all other oppressions. This is where we are first trained to be victims and oppressors.

Some of our personal struggles have been so persistent throughout our lives that we come to think of them as purely inborn personal defects. This is reinforced by a mental health system that primarily promotes a biological or genetic source to all human behaviour. In contrast to this, the viewpoint here is that many of these struggles have a social origin and are not necessarily permanent or unchange-able. We can heal these hurts and recover our connection to our humanity. To do this, it helps to understand how hurt affects us.

EFFECTS OF HURT

Normally, when we face a new situation that is non-threatening, our minds weigh it up and invent an appropriate, flexible response. We draw on our experience of similar situations, take account of how this new situation is different and come up with an appropriate way of dealing with it. We are able to vary how we react if the circumstances call for it. One of the key indications that someone is not struggling with hurt is the ability to be flexible in how they think and act.

When we get hurt, however, a number of things happen. One of these is that our ability to think clearly shuts down or, at least, does not function as well as before. We often hear people describe this. They say, *I was so scared, my mind went blank* or *I was so nervous, I couldn't think of anything to say* or *I was so angry, I couldn't put two words together*. Sometimes in a hurtful situation our thinking shuts down completely. Other times it doesn't completely shut down but seems to slow down so that we can't think fast enough to handle the situation.

A second effect of being hurt is that our judgement gets distorted. It becomes difficult to judge or make sense of what is happening around us. As a result, we may hear criticism where none is intended, or we may see a threat where there isn't any in reality. In a range of ways we misinterpret what people are saying or doing. We misread the situation. This, of course, is understandable if our ability to think clearly has been interfered with.

In a hurtful situation, therefore, two vital coping mechanisms stop working. We cannot think straight, and we are prone to misjudge what is happening and what the situation calls for. Under these circumstances, we have to handle the situation in some other way.

Usually, what we do is fall back on an automatic response that does not involve thinking. We react in ways we have done previously when faced with other hurtful situations. However, because our thinking machinery is not working properly, we fail to notice that this current situation is different and requires a different response. Our thinking has become rigid and our behaviour has become inflexible. It's as though, when we go into automatic mode, we fall back on an old habit that we developed a long time ago in situations somewhat similar to this.

The people around us who know us well may be very familiar with this old habit of ours. They know that if they say or do the wrong thing, we will go into automatic mode and react in very predictable ways. So they know that in certain situations we will flare up and react angrily, or we will go quiet, or we will withdraw and sulk, or we will freeze with terror, and so on. The effect of hurt, over time, is to leave us prone to act and think in rigid, predictable ways. And because these reactions are unthinking, they tend to be inappropriate. They are not flexible reactions to a new situation but rigid, habitual reactions to old situations that this new situation has reminded us of.

Sometimes we can recognise when this has happened to us. Painful feelings come up and we go into automatic mode. Afterwards, when the feelings have subsided, we may say, *I knew I shouldn't have said that, but I couldn't stop myself.* We know that what we said or did was inappropriate, but in the midst of the feelings we were unable to react in any other way.

Occasionally we can see this happen unexpectedly to others. We may be having a relaxed conversation with someone and suddenly we notice them starting to shut down. We see a particular look in their eyes or we detect a change in their tone of voice. We can see them disconnect from us and become rigid. At that point, nothing we say or do seems to get through to them.

One of the reasons why conflict escalates is that one or more of the parties involved has shut down and become unreachable. At times it can resemble two robots, in automatic mode, trading insults or threats. No one is able to listen or to think flexibly.

Under these circumstances, it is clear that some of the things we do to handle conflict simply don't work. In situations where someone has gone into automatic mode, it is pointless to try to reason or argue with them. Their thinking and judgement machinery is not working properly and they are unable to hear reason or logic.

These rigid, unthinking and inflexible habits arise for understandable reasons given the hurts we have experienced. They come to be seen as part of our personality. They can be changed, however;

they do not have to be permanent. It is possible to heal from the hurts that caused us to react like this.

THE HEALING PROCESS

Particularly since the 1950s and 1960s, with the development of various liberation movements, such as women's liberation, the civil rights movement, gay liberation and so on, we have learned much about how the damaging effects of oppression at a personal level can be healed and overcome.

Telling Our Story

When groups of women came together in the early days of the modern women's movement, they listened to one another's story. As they listened, they could hear echoes of their own story. There was a pattern to the stories that each woman could identify and resonate with. What had seemed like a purely individual experience bore a striking similarity to other women's experiences. As the stories unfolded there was a collective sense of relief as people realised *It's not just me*. The more they listened, the clearer it became that all these seemingly individual experiences were actually part of a larger system of oppression. Women could see that there was something going on here that was much bigger than any personal failing. The problem was not the person, it was the system around them. It was clear that instead of blaming themselves for their struggles they needed to focus on a system that was hugely oppressive. Listening to each other's story enabled them to name that system and describe in detail the many ways it damaged women.

As women listened to one another, a load began to lift from their shoulders. They no longer needed to give themselves a hard time because of the struggles they faced. It was not their fault. And as they listened more, they began to identify different ways that they could reclaim pride in themselves and be pleased with themselves as women, given what they had to struggle against. As their self-esteem grew, they also began to reclaim their power. Instead of seeing themselves simply as victims, or identifying themselves with their struggle, they began to challenge sexism and male domination and find new ways to act with power. Even though that oppressive system was still in place and they still faced big struggles, they were no longer just victims. A healing process was taking place that was transforming them at a personal and collective level and ultimately challenging and undermining the system of oppression that was at the heart of their struggle.

It is hard to overestimate the significance of the listening process. The women's movement is a powerful demonstration of the difference listening can make. And this is not confined to the women's movement. Since the 1950s, a similar process has taken place in a wide variety of other social groups. African heritage and Asian heritage people, for example, have been the target of white racism. As people from these groups came together to listen to one another, what had seemed like purely personal struggles were redefined as oppression directed against people because of their skin colour or their ethnicity and not because of any individual or personal defect. As people with a lesbian, gay or bisexual identity listened to one another, the workings of a systematic process of gay oppression became clear. As they continued to listen, this created space and safety for more specific identities to speak out – transgender, queer, intersex, and others.

This simple process of listening to other people who share the same identity or the same struggle is a powerful tool for healing. We see the evidence of it all around us. People with disabilities, elders, people of particular faiths, immigrants, survivors of the mental health system, lone parents and many others draw huge support from coming together and listening to each other's story. The effect is a general one – the focus shifts from self-blame to naming the ways that the personal struggle is rooted in an oppressive system.

The Discharge Process

Listening leads to profound change and healing. This can be enhanced by a deeper understanding of what happens when respectful and thoughtful listening takes place. When people feel safe and cared about, they are able not only to tell their story but also to feel all the feelings that are attached to that story. As the safety grows, they are able to release these feelings in ways that enhance the healing. This release is accompanied by particular expressions, particular ways the feelings show up or are vented, or particular ways they are discharged.

Some important things happen as feelings are discharged. Quite often, people will report that they don't feel as bad. For example, we might hear someone say they had been feeling sad or depressed but that after having a good cry they felt much better. People sometimes describe this as getting things out of their system. A more important effect, however, is that their thinking often changes. This is a complex process but it seems to be the case that, as we discharge our feelings, our ability to think is freed up. Where, before, our thinking was rigid or we had become inflexible, we can now think more clearly and react in a more flexible way.

This process of being able to think more clearly about situations happens automatically as we discharge. It is not a separate, conscious, intellectual process. It does not require anyone to analyse us or interpret our feelings. The discharge process seems to lead to a re-wiring of our brains so that afterwards we simply see things differently.

Releasing or discharging the feelings attached to our struggles can sometimes be confusing for us. We (or the people around us) may feel like we are 'falling apart', losing control or having a breakdown.

Mostly, however, the discharge process is the way in which human beings naturally heal from hurt. Rather than something to be feared, it is something to be welcomed. The more we understand this process, the easier it is to see its benefits. So let us look at some examples of how painful feelings are released and healed.

Grief

People who experience hurt of one kind or another accumulate grief. People who have been bereaved, or who have been hurt by others close to them, or who have witnessed people they care about being hurt, feel sadness, grief, pain, disappointment, and so on. They feel broken-hearted.

Often, the response of others to these feelings is to try to distract people or to encourage them to 'pull themselves together' or to reassure them. There may be some circumstances where these responses make sense. Mostly, however, what people need is the space and the safety to feel these feelings and let them out rather than bottle them up.

When we connect with and talk about our feelings of grief and hurt, typically we will shed tears. This sometimes confuses people. In an effort to be helpful, they may try to stop us crying. They act as though crying was the same as hurting, and believe that if they can stop the crying, that will stop the hurting. But in fact the crying is the healing of hurt, not the hurt itself. If we suppress the crying, we stop the healing.

We often see this happen around young children. When they experience hurt, their natural reaction is to cry. If we can resist the urge to stop them or distract them, children will cry until the hurt is gone. Afterwards, they will once again be relaxed, bright and free of the hurt. If we can provide safety and loving attention, the natural process of healing will occur and the child will be left with little or no residue of the hurt.

The confusion around this has meant that many adults had this natural healing process interfered with as they grew up. As children, when we cried the adults around us grew impatient or found the crying unbearable and tried to stop it. Some of us heard the refrain, *If you don't stop crying, I'll give you something to really cry about!* So we got hurt and then we got hurt again when we tried to heal.

The result of this is that the hurt remains undischarged and our ability to think and act flexibly in situations that resemble the original hurtful situation is interfered with. We don't think as well as we could and our behaviour becomes less flexible.

Faced with that reaction from the adults around us, some of us tried not to let our feelings show. This is difficult, however; it's hard to sit on feelings of hurt. Indeed many of us found that the only way we could not show feelings was to not let ourselves have those feelings in the first place. We went numb. We cut ourselves off from our feelings. When that happened, there was no healing and we became rigid and inflexible around that hurt.

This was particularly the case with boys and men. There was somewhat more slack in relation to girls that allowed them to show more of their feelings, especially what are sometimes called the softer feelings. For boys, however, early on they got the message that big boys don't cry. The result is that many males have difficulty connecting with their feelings and even more difficulty showing those feelings. While males were often discouraged from crying, females were often discouraged from showing anger or outrage. The oppression around gender had different effects on each group.

Fear

Many of us got hurt in situations that were frightening. We experienced violence or threats, sometimes as children and sometimes in later years as adults. Often, it was not safe to show how scared we were and we ended up holding in the fear. As a result, we may have become super-sensitive to danger and constantly alert to the possibility of violence or threat. Even relatively innocuous situations that have some vague resemblance to situations where we got hurt can bring up the fear.

In extreme situations, we can see how this fear takes over our bodies, our facial expressions and our voices. The locked-in fear has become chronic and is reflected in these various physical ways. The fear can be triggered by anything that reminds us of the original threatening situation, even if there is no actual danger in the present situation.

Our bodies have a natural way of dealing with fear and that is to shake. Sometimes this is accompanied by a cold sweat. One example of this was a parent in a war-torn country who described seeing their young baby lying in a cot shaking all over in the aftermath of a bombing. Shaking or trembling and sweating is the way we release and heal from fear. Here again, people can get confused. They think that the shaking is the same as the fear and if they can stop the shaking, that will stop the fear. In reality, if we stop the shaking, we lock in the fear.

If we can stay relaxed and provide safety, others will be able to feel their fear and shake as they describe what happened. When they know it is safe and that the person listening is not worried about them, they can tell their story. As they shake, they free themselves from the fear and reclaim their ability to think clearly about the frightening situation.

Embarrassment

Embarrassment is a form of light fear. Unlike heavy fear, embarrassment and other forms of light fear discharge through laughter. Laughter is the release and healing of light fear. It is not necessarily the case that there is something funny or amusing. In situations where people are tense, for example, laughter often leads to the release of that tension. We see this sometimes where someone cracks a joke when things get tense and everyone starts laughing.

In normal circumstances, that joke might not be particularly funny but in the tense situation it serves to trigger laughter. People feel less tense and less scared after the laughter. As they laugh, their thinking is freed up and they can see things more flexibly. To the extent that we can keep people laughing, the fear is released and their thinking becomes more relaxed.

Many people try to hold in their embarrassment by staying composed. Sometimes we see people who are rigidly composed and because of it are unable to show any spontaneity or other traces of humanity. This is sometimes a feature of oppressor groups and it can make it hard to be around them. To the extent that we can help them to laugh, the composure drops away and we begin to see the real human underneath that façade.

Anger/Outrage

Anger or outrage discharges through loud sounds, violent movements and warm sweat. We sometimes talk about people getting 'hot under the collar'. A classic example is a child having a tantrum.

Many of us struggle with listening to anger. Our own experience was probably that there was little slack among the people around us for our own anger. Our attempts to show our anger were silenced or we were punished for showing it. We may also have experienced hurt from people who looked and sounded angry at the time. So in the face of other people's anger we get scared.

There are many situations, however, where it is useful to encourage people to express what we could call righteous indignation about what they have experienced. Being able to stay with people while they show this anger can be hugely supportive. We might encourage them to direct their anger at us as a representative of those who hurt or oppressed them. Interestingly, if we can do this and welcome their anger, they will not be confused about us. They can use us as a target for their anger but behind this they are clear that we are actually an ally for them. So, for example, it can be very useful for a man to allow himself to be the butt of women's anger about sexism or male domination. It can be very useful for a white person to allow themselves to be the focus of a person of colour's anger about racism. If we can create the safety for people to show their anger, we can help to heal the hurt they have been carrying and enable them to have a different perspective on that hurt.

Similarly, it can be healing for us to release our own anger about what happened to us. If we can tell our story in a situation where those with us can stay relaxed in the face of our anger and encourage us to show it all, we can free ourselves from feelings that may have left us isolated, resentful or bitter.

It is important to note that there is a difference between the discharge of anger and the 'acting out' of anger. One difference is that discharge is not accompanied by violence or destructive behaviour.

Light Anger

Not all anger is extreme. We also experience light anger and this is generally released through laughter. We sometimes see this in confrontation situations where someone starts to get angry and begins to laugh. The laughter may seem misplaced but it is actually a form of discharge. Occasionally, it can be misinterpreted as mocking. In actual fact, to the extent that we can keep people laughing, they will free themselves from the anger.

Physical Tension

One other form of discharge is yawning. Yawning is the release of physical tension. When people tell their story, they may find a pull to yawn as they talk. This is actually very useful and we can encourage them to keep yawning as they talk. It is not simply that they are tired or haven't had enough sleep. Often people find themselves yawning in situations that are nervous or tense. Sometimes yawning will follow other forms of discharge, so that crying, for example, will give way to yawning. This is completely natural and is the body's way of healing itself.

Support Groups

In theory, it is possible that someone could discharge all of their painful feelings and free themselves from their hurts all on their own. This process works much better, however, when people get together with others in a support group for this purpose.

The listening that takes place in support groups can lead to the development of a social explanation for people's struggles. Hearing other people's stories allows us to see much more clearly how our struggles are part of a bigger system of oppression and not purely personal. We are able to describe, in great detail, how our struggles originate within that oppressive system, how they are maintained, and what needs to change if they are to be eliminated. As this understanding grows, it provides an alternative perspective on our struggles that enhances the listening and healing process. Once we understand social processes such as racism or sexism or ageism or homophobia and so on, we listen without believing there is something inherently wrong with the person. As we tell our own story, there is less of a pull to self-blame and a greater ability to discharge the feelings we have internalised that hitherto left us confused about ourselves.

For this reason, we have seen the emergence of a wide range of support groups in different settings, for example women's groups, men's groups, Traveller groups, LGBTQ+ groups, and so on. These groups work most effectively when the focus is on listening to one another rather than discussing or debating issues.

One of the lessons I have learned from working with a wide variety of groups is that discussion, as opposed to listening, often leads to confusion, disagreement and a lowering of safety. This is particularly the case when people with a mix of identities come together to discuss issues. So, for example, putting a diverse group of women and men together in a room to discuss gender equality or sexism can often be a recipe for disaster. Very quickly people become defensive or the discussion degenerates into banter and becomes trivialised. Sometimes they start to compete or to argue about which of them is more oppressed. Often there just isn't enough safety for people to keep listening to one another. For such meetings to work, it is necessary to have a very clear understanding of the dynamics of oppressed–oppressor communication and a set of ground rules to structure what happens.

There are two simple but powerful guidelines that facilitate a useful coming together of diverse groups. The first of these is that everyone gets equal time to talk, that no one person dominates the discussion. The second is that there is no comment or discussion after each person's contribution; all discussion is postponed until after everyone has spoken. The combined effect of these two guidelines is to create space and safety for each person to speak without interruption and without having to defend anything they say. The focus then goes on listening and understanding rather than arguing or debating. We can sometimes build on these two guidelines by agreeing that those from the oppressed group will speak first. There are other supplementary guidelines that can further enhance this process, but these two are the most important ones.

In certain situations, it is possible to have an even deeper listening in a diverse group. Once we understand the way oppressor groups tend to dominate and monopolise discussions, we can set it up to reverse that pattern. In this case, we agree that the only people who will speak will be those from the oppressed group and that those from the oppressor group will simply listen without comment.

One of the most powerful meetings I have ever facilitated was where a group of men and women came together and I asked the women how they had experienced sexism or male domination in their lives. The job of the men at this meeting was just to listen. After a slight hesitation, the women began to take it in turns to talk about their experiences. By the time the last woman had spoken, everyone in the room was deeply moved, including the men. The women were touched by each other's stories but also inspired by their ability to name the oppression. The men learned more about women's oppression than had been possible in any discussion they had ever had. More importantly, they got a clear picture of the work they had to do as men in order to be effective allies for women. We finished up by having the women meet in groups of two or three and the men do likewise, with each group discussing among themselves the feelings that came up for them in the meeting.

The structure of that meeting was unusual and might, at first glance, seem unfair because only one group got to speak. In the context of oppression, however, creating opportunities like this for an oppressed group to be listened to without interruption, without comment and without argument is a powerful learning experience and an extremely empowering one for the oppressed group. It can evoke strong feelings for the oppressor group who are listening and they then get to work on and process these feelings when they meet together on their own. This works extremely well when the people from the oppressor group are committed to being good allies for the oppressed group, when they are clear that they are not oppressed by the oppressed group and are in fact in the oppressor role, and when they have worked enough on themselves to have a clear sense of their own goodness and to have built close relationships with other people from their oppressor group.

In general, however, the listening process works best when people meet separately in their respective support groups rather than all together in the same group. This creates greater safety for people to speak openly and honestly and it means they don't have to worry about the effects of what they say on people with a different identity.

In fact, there is a principle that says, if you want to build unity across diverse identities, then first of all meet separately. Unfortunately, what often happens is that people from the oppressed group meet together but people from the oppressor group who are their allies never meet on their own and therefore never get to work together on their patterns of internalised domination. We shall see more on this below.

Overcoming Internalised Domination

Just as we can use telling our story, listening and discharging our feelings to heal the hurts associated with being oppressed, so also can we use these processes to free ourselves from internalised domination. Within our oppressor identities we have internalised all sorts of blocks and prejudices towards people from particular oppressed groups. These blocks and prejudices stifle our own growth and development and prevent us from having relaxed, non-oppressive, peer relationships with many of the people around us. As we take on the work of overcoming our internalised domination, we begin to see the extent to which our lives are deeply degraded by not having close relationships with the full diversity of humanity around us.

Safety and Honesty

Two particular conditions make it easier for us to eliminate the blocks and prejudices that interfere with our relationships. The first is having a safe place to show the feelings we have internalised. This is easier once we remember that no one is born oppressive and that underneath our patterns of domination we are completely good people. We can make it safe for people to show their prejudices without getting confused about their basic goodness.

The second condition is deciding to be completely honest about the thoughts and feelings that we carry. There is a way in which we often tiptoe around our prejudices, trying not to let them show. We keep our distance from people or we censor what's going on inside us. Unfortunately, it's almost impossible to hide this stuff. People from oppressed groups can spot patterns of internalised domination that we think we have kept hidden. Their antennae for these patterns are finely tuned. Not owning up to them or trying to keep them hidden actually holds them in place, makes it more likely that we will act them out, and prevents us from becoming free of them. It turns out that the way to get rid of these patterns is to talk honestly about them.

If we can be listened to respectfully while we talk about our oppressive thoughts, feelings and behaviour, they begin to lose their hold on us. If we can discharge the feelings of grief, fear and hurt that we experience as we talk about this, the more powerful the process becomes. One very useful way to begin is to talk about early memories associated with particular groups. For example, as a white person, I can talk about my early memories associated with people of a different skin colour and the feelings attached to these memories. I can tell the story of how these thoughts and feelings came about.

This works even better if I can do this with people who share the same oppressor identity. So as well as telling my own story, I get to listen to other white people telling their stories. You might think that doing this would have the opposite effect and reinforce our prejudices, but if we are clear about the process, this does not happen. One of the things that can happen is that, as I listen to other white people, for example, the prejudices gradually seem ridiculous. When people speak honestly and from the heart, it becomes clear that the patterns of domination sit on top of our own hurts and have nothing to do with the reality of other groups. As a man, for example, the more I look at how I act out sexism the more I can see how it is connected to my own feelings of fear, loneliness and isolation.

One very important thing to remember here, as we saw above, is that it doesn't work well if we try to do this in mixed groups. There isn't enough safety and it brings up too many feelings for people from the oppressed group to have to listen to what we have internalised as oppressors. They experience enough of that in their day-to-day lives without having to be a listener while people from the oppressor group try to work through their feelings. Occasionally, an oppressed person who has worked a lot on their own feelings may choose to listen to the oppressor, but it doesn't work to expect or require this as part of the healing process for oppressor groups.

We do not see many examples of this process among oppressor groups. We do not often see groups of white people coming together to discharge and heal from their racism. We do not see groups of settled people working on their prejudices towards Travellers. We do not see groups of heterosexuals looking at their internalised homophobia. We do see it sometimes with groups of men coming together to work on sexism. Unfortunately, though, confusion about how oppression works and about the healing process has led some of these men's groups to shift from being allies of women to seeing women or feminism as the problem.

It can be painful and requires a lot of honesty to face the feelings of being an oppressor. And it requires a deep understanding of the dynamics of oppressed–oppressor relationships and the skills to facilitate safety, good listening and honesty. What sometimes happens is that people with oppressor identities who want to be good allies for people from the oppressed group focus instead on becoming aware of all the ways the oppression affects the oppressed group. They tend not to look at themselves and their own oppressive behaviour. In doing this, they try to keep their own oppressive thoughts and feelings out of sight and under control. This works up to a point but it often leads to confusion and unaware oppressiveness. One simple example of that is where these well-intentioned allies end up taking over leadership of social change organisations or lobby groups instead of following the leadership of people from the oppressed group. It is not uncommon to see groups that represent oppressed people being led by well-meaning people from the oppressor group. Unless we are discharging regularly on our own oppressor patterns, we will inadvertently slip into being oppressive even in situations where we are trying to help.

The challenge for any kind of progressive group or organisation is to create opportunities for people to be listened to within their own identity groups. This would include meetings of people with the same oppressed identity and meetings of allies who have the oppressor identity. Periodically, these groups could also come together to listen (without discussion) to what they have been learning about themselves in their respective groups.

CONCLUSION

Telling our story, accompanied by discharge of painful feelings where appropriate, is central to the healing process. Apart from the release of tension and the freeing up of our thinking, it allows us to separate our pain and our struggles from what is true of us inherently as human beings. It enables us to locate the source of our struggles outside of ourselves rather than seeing them as a personal failing or flaw. Instead of seeing the discharge of painful feelings as something gone wrong or an indication we are 'cracking up', we can see them as natural reactions to pain and opportunities for healing if handled thoughtfully.

Questions

1. How easy or difficult is it for you to feel and discharge the different kinds of painful feelings described in this chapter?

2. What messages did you get growing up about showing your feelings?

CHAPTER 5

The Liberation Process

n the previous chapter, we saw how individuals can heal from the hurts they have experienced. They do this by sharing and listening to one another's stories and discharging the feelings associated with those stories. In doing this together, people see how their individual struggles are actually shared struggles to a great extent. What feels like a purely personal experience turns out to be one that many others also struggle with. So not only does this become a healing process, it also becomes a consciousness-raising process. Going hand-in-hand with the healing is a growing awareness of how an oppressive system contributed to the hurt and how it continues to perpetuate that hurt for many people.

In this way, the healing process becomes part of an even bigger process of liberation from oppression. It is clear that, if we do not eliminate the oppressions that are the source of most of the hurt that people struggle with, then these hurts continue to be passed on and the healing can never be complete. Fortunately, we can learn from various attempts to overcome oppressive systems and describe how the liberation process works.

STAGES OF LIBERATION

Looked at from the point of view of the oppressed group, we can think of the liberation process as moving through four stages (see Figure 5 below).

Stage 1: Oppressed

The first stage in this process is really a pre-liberation stage. This is where the oppression is widespread and largely unquestioned in any systematic or organised way, even though there may be some individuals and groups who try to challenge the oppression on the fringes. People are mistreated physically, economically, sexually, socially or psychologically and this is tolerated or even encouraged within the wider society. Because of the way oppression becomes internalised, as we saw in Chapter 3, even those who are on the receiving end of the oppression may come to accept it as inevitable, unchangeable, deserved, or part of the natural order of things. Regardless of the hurt, inequality or damage that they suffer, they feel powerless to change anything. They are encouraged to be subservient, dependent on the goodwill of the oppressor group, undemanding or even invisible, and accepting of their second-class status.

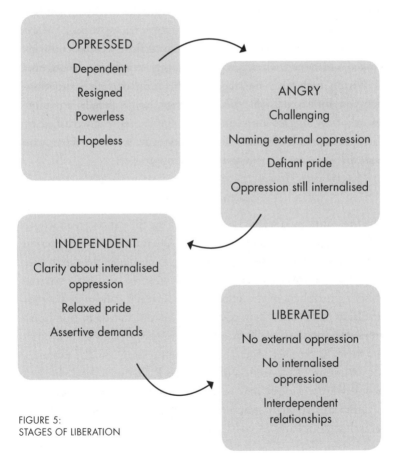

FIGURE 5:
STAGES OF LIBERATION

Assimilation is also a characteristic of this stage. People try to fit in to the dominant culture by giving up significant aspects of their own culture such as their language, religion, dress, food, traditions, and so on. They may be encouraged to look down on these aspects of their own culture and may want their children to take on the language and culture of the oppressor group and model themselves on that group.

The oppressor group, on the other hand, are seen by themselves, and often by members of the oppressed group, as superior, entitled to privilege or 'normal'. People from this group are looked up to, admired or envied. Their values, beliefs, assumptions, opinions, behaviour and lifestyles become the standards against which people are judged and valued. They become the group to aspire to belong to.

Within each of these stages of liberation there are variations between individuals. At this first stage, some people are more aware of the oppression than others. Some feel more crushed by the oppression than others. In a general way, however, there is no widespread or overt challenging of the oppression.

Stage 2: Angry

The first, oppressed stage may last for a long time and vary in length from one oppressed group to another. The transition to the second stage depends on something happening to challenge the status quo.

Sometimes this may occur as a result of some glaring or extreme abuse of members of the oppressed group that galvanises people's revulsion and shakes them out of their apathy, inertia or numbness around the oppression. There may be a triggering event that becomes the focus of people's anger about the oppression. So, for example, the execution of the leaders of the 1916 Rising in Ireland shocked people who previously may have been apathetic or even hostile and gave rise to a strongly supported independence movement. Or the refusal of Rosa Parks to give up her seat on a bus to a white person became a symbol of the oppression of African Americans and an inspiration for change.

In other situations, there may not be one particular trigger but rather a general change in society that leads to changes in people's perception of what is acceptable. Access to education is one such change. Information about other liberation movements is another, perhaps as a result of education or greater media coverage. Within this changing social environment, visionary or charismatic leaders often emerge who are able to articulate the suffering of their people and hold out a vision of a non-oppressive society. We can think of people like Martin Luther King, Nelson Mandela, Mahatma Gandhi, and many others. What they have in common is their success in articulating grievances and mobilising opposition to the oppression.

This second stage is labelled *Angry* because it is often characterised by the release of pent-up anger about the oppression. Whereas before, most people accepted or endured the oppression without overt opposition or questioning, now there is a widespread, organised, angry denunciation of the ways people have been victimised and demands for an end to the inequality.

The relationship with members of the oppressor group changes here also. It now becomes more negative or more charged with resentment or suspicion. Where before people admired, aspired to be like, or saw themselves as inferior to the dominant group, they now identify members of the oppressor group as the source of their oppression and see them, to one degree or another, as the enemy. At Stage 1, members of the oppressed group may have been at pains not to question or challenge members of the oppressor group or may even have tried to reassure them that they were not being oppressive. At Stage 2, this changes. The oppression is now being directly challenged and the oppressed group is no longer concerned to protect the feelings of the oppressor group.

There are also changes in how people feel about their identity. Instead of feeling ashamed of who they are, they now consciously claim and take pride in their oppressed identity. The characteristics that previously were looked down on or stereotyped, such as the way they spoke or their appearance, now become the focus of this pride. People begin to turn what were once insulting or negative terms into badges of pride. So at this stage we hear phrases like 'Black is Beautiful' or 'Gay Pride'. Women claim to be 'Fully Female in Every Fibre'. People also begin to take a very positive interest in their culture and their language instead of assimilating into the dominant culture. They now put their own name on their identity rather than accepting the labels of the oppressor group. So, for example, they identify as Travellers rather than itinerants. They are women rather than girls.

Internalised Oppression

An important aspect of this stage is that the oppressed group, perhaps for the first time, is naming the oppression and spelling out the different ways it victimises them. However, while they are becoming clearer about the nature of the oppression and many of its effects, they tend not to be as clear about the way the oppression has been internalised. They can name the external oppression but not its internalised forms. This means that much of their resistance is coming from inside the internalised oppression.

We can see this sometimes in the type of pride that the group takes in itself. Rather than being a relaxed pride in their goodness, their humanity and other inherently human characteristics, the pride may be a reflection of the oppression. So, for example, Irish people may take pride in having endured eight hundred years of oppression or people may take pride in being survivors of abuse. Sometimes there may be a tendency to romanticise the oppressed culture as a contradiction to the shame people may have felt before. The pride, at this stage, is based on, or is a function of, the oppression rather than being completely outside it. It still defines itself relative to the former oppressor group. There may be an element of comparison with the oppressor group so that people take pride in being morally superior to their oppressors. They may only be able to feel good to the extent that they can see the oppressor as inherently bad or evil.

The various aspects of internalised oppression that we saw in Chapter 3 are still affecting them. This internalised oppression influences and shapes the way they fight the oppression and their ability to unite in opposition to it. Although they hold out a defiant pride, they still do not feel completely good about themselves or their people. While in their heads they reject the stereotypes, at an emotional level they still struggle with feelings of shame or inferiority. Although they are now organising to fight the oppression, they still carry feelings of powerlessness and hopelessness.

Also, although they see the oppressor group as the source of their difficulties, the struggle for liberation may be weakened by the emergence of different factions within the oppressed group who are hostile to or suspicious of one another. They struggle to form a united front and instead fight among themselves. In addition, they may find it hard to support their own leaders and may treat them with distrust or hostility.

Violence

As the oppression continues and particularly if the oppressive system resists change and attempts to suppress dissent, more militant or separatist groups of one kind or another may emerge at this stage. These groups may see the solution to the oppression as getting rid of those whom they perceive to be the enemy or, at least, distancing themselves from them. They see other people rather than oppressive systems as the source of their oppression. Some may try to target the oppressor group with violence and may adopt armed struggle as the strategy for achieving liberation, alongside militant political and social activism.

In thinking about this stage, it helps to understand how violence comes about. In general, violence seems to have three broad sources. One is the violence of the oppressor group that sits on top of their internalised domination. Feelings of superiority, entitlement and prejudice along with fear of the oppressed can lead oppressor groups to use violence to maintain the status quo. The well-known quotation that 'power corrupts and absolute power corrupts absolutely' captures some of this. As we saw in Chapter 2, violence may only need to be used occasionally as long as the oppressed group accepts its victim status. However, as resistance to the oppression grows, this particular violence may become more prevalent and come much more into the open.

A second source of violence is what we could call displaced violence. In this case, people who feel oppressed in particular ways may seek relief from their oppression by finding groups that they themselves can oppress. When we looked at the various aspects of internalised oppression in Chapter 3, we saw how an oppressive system encourages people to seek relief by targeting some other oppressed group. Rather than trying to eliminate their own oppression they are encouraged to direct their anger and frustration at another oppressed group that they can feel superior to. We can see this in the rise of populist movements that target immigrants, Muslims, asylum seekers or refugees as the source of difficulties facing the larger population.

A third source of violence that is particularly relevant at this stage of liberation is somewhat similar to that second source. In this case, however, feelings of powerlessness and hopelessness about their oppression lead people to resort to violence against the oppressor group as opposed to other oppressed groups. As the oppression begins to be named and the oppressor group identified, the violence becomes focused in that direction. (This is not to say that all violent resistance to oppression is rooted in powerlessness and hopelessness. There may be some situations where this is the only rational response.)

At this stage of the liberation process, however, people from the oppressor group are seen as the problem and violence against them is seen by some as the only solution.

The important thing to understand here is that when we look at oppressed groups, their violence often sits on feelings of powerlessness and hopelessness. Contrary to what the dominant groups often claim, the violence is rarely as simple as being the work of psychopaths or fanatics. Unfortunately, the reactions of the system in denying the reality of the oppression and refusing to make significant change reinforce the sense of desperation that people feel and therefore the pull to violent methods. This can create a cycle of violence-suppression-violence that may take years to overcome. We can see this in many conflicts around the world. Unless the underlying oppression is addressed, the violence continues.

Acknowledging this link between powerlessness and violence is not meant to justify violence or other activities that can also result from these feelings such as racketeering, robbery, drug-dealing or other destructive actions. But it does mean understanding these things in the context of oppression and internalised oppression rather than in a context of evil, immaturity or madness. Referring back to the earlier quotation, it is not only power that corrupts but also powerlessness. Extremes of power or powerlessness can lead to violence.

Occasionally, in the case of some national liberation movements for example, the violence leads to the overthrow of the dominant oppressor group. People may gain political independence that can then be confused with liberation. We see this in situations where, following independence, the internalised divisiveness comes to the surface and civil war breaks out. Or, having ousted a foreign power, the new people in power become almost as oppressive as those they had got rid of. Someone has described national independence as the right to be oppressed by your own people rather than foreigners. What this demonstrates is that removing the external oppression is not the same as liberation. Until the underlying internalised oppression is dealt with, there cannot be full liberation. What also happens is that various oppressed groups within a country, such as women for example, are persuaded to join the fight for independence with the promise of change when independence is gained. Following independence, however, the commitments made to these groups are reneged on and their oppression continues unabated. Here again, the failure to understand that full liberation cannot happen without the liberation of everyone eventually leads to the resumption of oppression in the new system.

Empowerment

The other side to this story is that people who feel powerful tend not to resort to violence. In a curious way, the solution to violence is to empower people. It may seem counter-intuitive to increase the power of people who are adopting violent methods but this is actually entirely logical. Where people feel powerful and can see themselves making progress, they generally do not resort to violence. We see examples of this in various political and labour struggles where groups that were highly militant or violent changed their strategies as they gained greater access to power and influence. For example, one of the major contributions to the peace process in Ireland was the removal of the ban on access to the mass media by members of Sinn Féin, the political wing of the IRA.

For this reason, the outrage people feel about their oppression does not necessarily lead to violent resistance. This is only one of the possibilities at Stage 2. Many other people may be angry but not violent. During this second stage, there are also movements of organised, non-violent action and attempts to raise awareness of the oppression through the media and other avenues. Sometimes a non-violent and a violent movement operate in parallel. As the non-violent approach becomes stronger and gains more access to channels of influence and as people begin to see things change, the support for armed struggle begins to wane.

Finally, we saw in the previous chapter how the feelings about oppression can be healed through listening and discharge. This also applies at this angry stage. Where people are listened to and have their feelings acknowledged, they can discharge the angry feelings rather than act them out. However, because it can be difficult to listen to anger, especially if the listener is a member of the oppressor group, this listening does not always happen. People try to deny or defend the oppression or shift the blame back on to the oppressed group. This leads to desperation among the oppressed group and increased feelings of powerlessness that can fuel violence. To the extent that we can provide opportunities for this listening to take place and support for the people in their struggles, the anger can be channelled into more empowering and effective strategies for change.

Stage 3: Independent

Over time, people work through the anger, discharge it and leave it behind. This stage represents a change in how people see themselves and members of oppressor groups and a change in their relationships. They are no longer operating largely from inside their internalised oppression. The pride that they now have is not based on enduring or surviving oppression nor on comparing themselves with their oppressors. Rather, it is a pride in positive, human qualities such as their intelligence, their goodness, their courage, their strength, their power, their creativity, the richness of their culture, and so on. Whereas before they may have depended on their relationship with members of the oppressor group for their self-esteem and their sense of identity, now they are independent of that group. Whether or not they have people from that group in their lives is irrelevant to them; what people from that group think of them doesn't matter.

In the past, they may have sought to be close to people from the oppressor group or may have tried to look good in their eyes. These are no longer that important to them. The relationship is one of independence.

At this stage, people are also much clearer about how the oppression became internalised and the effects that it had on them. A lot of the anger they felt as victims has passed, to be replaced by a sense of righteous indignation. They are now much more assertive rather than aggressive or violent. Now they expect things to change and be made right.

At the angry stage, people would have been inclined to see the oppressor group as the enemy. At Stage 3, they see the oppressive system rather than other people as the enemy. They can see that while that system functions in ways that are oppressive, unequal, destructive and demeaning, there are people in the oppressor group who are opposed to this and who try to be allies and supports for the people who are oppressed. Because of their conditioning to be oppressive, these people may still behave inappropriately at times but they are trying to be more aware and to act outside this conditioning. For this reason, people from the oppressed group may have good relationships with individuals from the oppressor group while being very clear that the oppression still exists and has to change.

Progress through these various stages is not even. At any given time, some people may still be stuck at Stage 1. Others may be at an angry Stage 2, while some may have moved past this to an independent, assertive Stage 3. We can think about individuals and where they are on this journey and we can think about whole groups and where they are. At particular points, the bulk of people and groups may be at one of the stages while a minority may be at an earlier or later stage. Being able to see this as a series of stages rather than a set of fixed, unchanging reactions helps us to think more clearly about what we see happening around us.

In many ways, the modern women's movement is the most advanced liberation movement we have seen. Many women's groups and individual women operate at the third stage. They have reclaimed a relaxed pride in who they are along with a deep sense of their inherent power. While the oppression is still in place, they are much less confused by the internalised oppression and very clear about the external oppression.

It can also happen that, at this third stage, people begin to feel that the oppression is over. At a personal level they feel more confident and powerful and some of the extremes of the external oppression have become less prevalent or visible. In the case of women, some come to believe that sexism and male domination are no longer an issue. And, of course, the oppressive system will encourage this belief. In reality, however, at this stage the oppression is still operating. It may be less obvious or changes may have occurred more in some places compared to others but the system of oppression is still largely intact. In the face of liberation movements it may have adapted to become more subtle, or cosmetic changes may have occurred to make it appear that people have more freedom than they actually have. The oppression still continues, however. What characterises this third stage is a change within the oppressed group rather than the removal of the system of oppression.

It should be noted that all through this process the oppressive system will find ways to monitor, disrupt, discredit and make money from liberation movements. In particular, the use of social media provides enormous access to personal information that can be used to track individuals and groups, identify their interests and political leanings, influence their thinking and understanding of what's happening in the world, and enable market researchers to target popular movements as potential sources of profit by manipulating their slogans, ideals and vision.

Stage 4: Liberated

At the fourth stage of this process, the actual system of oppression is dismantled. Both the external oppression and the internalised oppression have been eliminated. In addition, there has been a complete change within the oppressor group. Not only do they no longer act out the oppression, all of the internalised domination is gone. They no longer carry feelings of superiority or entitlement or prejudice and their relationship with the oppressed group is now one of true equality.

At this stage, the various identities that people have no longer have great significance and they are free to discard them. They have worked through the hurts, eliminated the oppression and reclaimed their full humanity. These identities don't serve any purpose or mean much now. At last, they can relate to one another simply as humans.

For a variety of reasons, this final stage is purely theoretical. In reality, this has never happened. We have no examples of the complete elimination of the oppression of a group. Movements such as women's liberation have sometimes come close but women's oppression has not ended so far.

For this stage to be reached, the system has to change to reflect the complete humanness and equality of the oppressed group. For that to happen, the oppressor group has to be freed from its internalised oppression and domination. Because of the way in which different oppressions interlink, overlap and hold one another in place, reaching Stage 4 would require the elimination of these other oppressions at the same time. In a very real way, the liberation of any one group requires the liberation of all groups.

So, for example, we cannot fully achieve women's liberation until we have men's liberation. The latter would free men from their isolation and disconnection from feelings as well as the superiority and other patterns of domination that they may be prone to, and at the same time enable them to reconnect with their inherent goodness and worth. We cannot have these liberations until we have gay liberation. This, in turn, requires the elimination of racism and class oppression, and so on. Each liberation rests on the other liberations. All of these require the ending of the oppression of children and young people, since this is where the process of oppression begins and where, effectively, we train people to become oppressed victims and oppressors.

The trend of human development over time has been to move in the direction of this final stage, but the belief that this could be achieved is often dismissed as pure idealism. However, our sense of hopefulness about achieving this ideal is easily distorted by our continued internalised oppression. It is important that we separate our feelings of discouragement and hopelessness about the possibility of eliminating oppression from a rational decision to work towards that goal. Most of our discouragement and hopelessness are the result of our internalised oppression and are therefore not a good guide to what it is possible to achieve.

OPPRESSOR LIBERATION

Just as we can describe the stages of liberation from oppression, so we can also describe a similar or parallel set of stages of oppressor liberation (Figure 6). This has similarities to the stages of cultural competency that we saw in Chapter 2.

Stage 1: Oppressing

At this stage, the oppression is strongly in place. Members of the dominant, oppressor group display arrogance, superiority and a sense of entitlement to privilege. They take this privilege and their power within the system for granted and see no reason to question or challenge the status quo. Attempts to be progressive result, at best, in a type of benign paternalism that keeps members of the oppressed group in a state of dependency. Progressive members of the oppressor group fail to notice the many subtle ways in which they continue to communicate their belief in their own superiority and entitlement to privilege.

Stage 2: Denial

This stage represents a response to protests and opposition from the oppressed group. There is an initial feeling of shock and disbelief that anyone would question the way things are. Some members of the group feel hurt by accusations that their behaviour and attitudes are oppressive. They believe they have not acted in any overtly oppressive ways with violence or abuse and struggle to see how, in other more subtle ways, their behaviour and attitudes are patronising or otherwise oppressive. Others react angrily and defiantly and are outraged at the criticism and demands of the oppressed group. They use their power to suppress dissatisfaction or dissent and attack those who are promoting change. The efforts of the oppressed group to claim and take pride in their own identity are somehow seen as an attack on the dominant group. Men, for example, may feel very threatened by women who feel good about being female, who like themselves and other women, and who do not look to men to meet their needs. Their independence may be interpreted as an attack on men or as man-hating. In response to these changes among the oppressed group, members of the oppressor group may take a defiant pride in the symbols of their power and privilege and portray themselves as victims rather than perpetrators. This stage may be characterised by an angry and sometimes violent backlash against members of the oppressed group and a blaming of this group for their own disadvantaged circumstances.

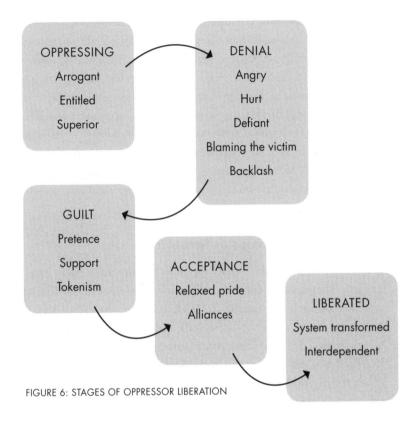

FIGURE 6: STAGES OF OPPRESSOR LIBERATION

Stage 3: Guilt

While some individuals and groups within the wider oppressor group may get stuck at Stage 2, others may move on to Stage 3. Here there is some recognition and acceptance that oppression exists. People can see in a broad way that the other group has been mistreated and feel guilty about what has happened to them. However, they have difficulty seeing the full extent and effects of the oppression and difficulty seeing how their own personal behaviour, attitudes or relationships are part of the oppression. They may talk the language of equality or justice or liberation but there is considerable unaware pretence in the positions they take. They support equality in theory but this is not fully reflected in their behaviour. The guilt that some people feel may lead them to try to reverse roles, perhaps acting submissively around the oppressed group or romanticising that group. The effect of this on people from the oppressed group is generally not very positive. Others may make token efforts to change the situation but they still operate out of feelings of superiority, fear or entitlement. While they are aware of the oppressiveness of the system, they tend to be unaware of their own personal internalised domination and how this shapes their reactions.

Stage 4: Acceptance

Over time, some members of the oppressor group move on to Stage 4. Here there is an acceptance of their own oppressor conditioning and the need for both personal and system change. The earlier defiant pride that clung rigidly to the beliefs and symbols of domination is now replaced with a relaxed pride in their own basic humanity that does not depend on comparison with or superiority over any other group. At this stage, there are two aspects to their response. On the one hand, they are actively working to overcome their own prejudices and eliminate the traces of internalised domination. This includes working to raise the awareness of other members of their oppressor group about the oppression and its effects. On the other hand, they are also building alliances with members of the oppressed group in an effort to change the oppressive system. They recognise the limitations imposed on their thinking and awareness by their oppressor conditioning and allow themselves to be guided by the thinking and awareness of the oppressed group. This includes supporting and following the leadership of members of the oppressed group.

Stage 5: Liberated

As with the earlier stages of liberation from oppression, the final stage of this process is, at this point, largely theoretical. Stage 5 requires the elimination of the oppression and the transformation of the oppressive system to one characterised by respect and equality. Patterns of internalised domination have been eliminated also and replaced with thoughtful, fulfilling and interdependent relationships.

Eliminating internalised domination is harder in some ways than eliminating internalised oppression. It tends to be more unaware of itself, and the privileges of domination provide little urgency to work for change. It is easier for people to fool themselves into believing everything is okay or that they do not carry oppressive feelings or attitudes than to make the changes necessary to eradicate oppression. Working through these stages of oppressor liberation requires a degree of humility and an openness to being guided and led by the oppressed group.

CONCLUSION

Human liberation moves through a series of stages, starting from within the oppression and gradually reclaiming our power, our pride and our connection to our inherent human qualities. In the case of oppressor groups, this process involves a recognition of the oppressive ways in which we act towards oppressed groups and the various ways in which we have been disconnected from our inherent human qualities. As oppressed and oppressor groups reclaim their humanity they can then work together to eliminate the oppressive system. Full liberation requires that we not only reclaim our human qualities and become allies for one another but that we finally change the system that keeps the oppression in place.

The liberation process represents a recognition that what we thought of as purely personal struggles are, in fact, collective struggles. As we come to see this, we also realise that the healing process is not just a personal journey. Healing takes place most fully when we join with others to challenge and change the social conditions that created our struggles in the first place. The oppressive system will try to individualise and medicalise our struggles and offer a combination of drug- and individual-focused therapies that leave social structures unchanged. Healing and liberation go hand in hand and represent a reclaiming of our connection to inherent human qualities that we have lost touch with. In a real sense, we discover there is actually nothing at all wrong with us. Underneath the oppressions that we have endured, we are completely okay. Our goodness is undiminished. We are smarter than we realise and, if people knew what we have had to handle in our lives, they could only be filled with admiration for how well we have done under those circumstances. We move from blaming ourselves for our struggles to seeing clearly that the fault lies not with us but with an oppressive system that damages people deeply and, finally, to taking active steps to eliminate that oppression.

Questions

1. In relation to an oppressed identity that you carry, what stage of liberation have you reached?

2. In relation to an oppressor identity that you carry, what stage of liberation have you reached?

3. What needs to change for you or your people to move to the next stage of liberation?

CHAPTER 6

Taking Charge of Our Struggles

So far, we have seen how struggle becomes part of our lives and the effects it can have. We have also seen how a lot of what we struggle with is rooted in broader processes of oppression. We looked at how we can heal the hurts associated with oppression and, in Chapter 5, we saw what is involved in liberating ourselves from those oppressions. Let's now look at what it means at a personal level to take charge of handling our struggles.

THREE IMPORTANT DECISIONS

We can think of three important decisions in the process of taking charge of our struggles. The goal is not so much to eliminate struggle but to get to a place where it does not overwhelm us or leave us feeling victimised or even to a place where tackling our struggle allows us to grow and reconnect with our inherent human strengths. Implicit in much of what we have looked at so far is the importance and the power of making decisions about what we struggle with.

1: Deciding What Is True of Me Inherently

In Chapter 1 we saw that there are particular qualities or traits that are part of human nature. These qualities include being intelligent, loving (and loveable), creative, powerful, cooperative, and with the capacity to enjoy life. Qualities such as these are universal. They apply to everyone, by nature. In a loose way, we can say that each one of us comes into the world with all of these qualities intact. Of course, we often don't feel that these qualities are part of our inherent nature. And we don't always see them reflected in other people. In the previous chapters, however, we saw how the experience of hurt and oppression has the effect of cutting us off from being able to appreciate these qualities in ourselves or drawing on them in our day-to-day life.

Faced with messages that I am inadequate, stupid, inferior, insignificant, or powerless to change anything, the first decision I can make is to reject these messages as an inaccurate description of me and my relationship to the people around me. This means that:

• I can decide to trust and believe in my intelligence, my goodness, my worth and my power regardless of what others say or even what my own feelings tell me.

• In the face of how bad I am feeling, I can decide to act on the assumption that I am a completely good person.

• I can decide to act in ways that I know make sense rather than go with what my worst feelings are telling me. In spite of everything, I do not have to be governed by my hurts and the ways they have left me feeling.

• I can understand that I am not my hurts. These do not have to define who I am or how I act.

So I can decide, for example, that *from this moment on, I will at all times act on the assumption that I am completely good, completely lovable and completely worthwhile*. Making decisions like this without reservation helps to balance the weight of the conditioning to feel bad about ourselves.

2: Deciding To Contradict My Internalised Oppression

Earlier, we saw how internalised oppression completely distorts our beliefs about ourselves and our people. As we become more aware of this, we can see particular beliefs and feelings attached to the different identities we carry. On a good day, we can see how these beliefs and feelings hold us back and interfere with our relationships. We can decide to do something about that.

So the second important decision I can make is to 'contradict' my internalised oppression. Contradicting means rejecting the negative messages I got and refusing to treat them as though they were true. It also means adopting a different attitude to, or perspective on, myself and acting in ways that go against how I was conditioned to behave by the oppression. What this might mean in practice will vary depending on the particular oppression and the messages that went with it. We saw examples of this in the last chapter with the slogans that different protest movements adopt, such as 'Black is Beautiful' or 'Gay Pride'.

An important part of contradicting the internalised oppression is deciding to claim my identity with pride, as we saw in Chapter 1. Because of how the oppression left me feeling, I might be inclined to hide my identity or have difficulty feeling good about it. Instead, however, I can embrace it and decide to stand proudly visible in this identity.

So, I can think of a particular oppressed identity that I have and notice the feelings attached to it. I now decide that *from this moment on, I will never again apologise for who I am. I will take pride in my identity and in my people and never allow shame to distort how I think or act. I will be pleased with myself at all times and expect others to treat me with complete respect.* Knowing how the internalised oppression pulls me to think, act and feel, I can decide to go in the exact opposite direction.

Here again, in contradicting internalised oppression it is usually helpful to do this without reservation. So it's not just that I am not inferior, it's that I am completely worthwhile. It's not just that I'm not a bad person, it's that I am completely good. In order to counterbalance the weight of the conditioning we received we have to hold a point of view that pushes us outside the comfort zone that we have become used to.

3: Deciding To Reclaim My Power

Over and above reconnecting with our inherent human qualities and contradicting our internalised oppression, it's also important that we actively do something. The third important decision is to reclaim my power. This means taking action, taking initiative and leadership. This can involve lots of different things in practice.

- I can change my personal life, in big or small ways.

- I can look after my health better.

- I can cut down on or cut out things that have a bad effect on me.

- I can get more exercise.

- I can get more rest.

- I can go after what's missing in my life.

- I can have more friends and have more fun in my life.

- I can move away from relationships that are destructive.

- I can find ways to be creative and express myself through art, craftwork, music, writing, dance, acting and look for ways to enjoy the creativity of others.

I can also challenge oppression and work for liberation. To the extent that we learn to live with oppression, or accept it as inevitable or as being too big to overcome, we are giving up our power. Part of overcoming our struggles is a decision to go after a bigger life that has liberation from oppression as a core piece. A useful way to look at this is in terms of taking leadership.

LEADERSHIP

Taking leadership is a powerful form of personal development. In order to be effective we have to step through any doubts or other feelings that hold us back, and to confront our internalised oppression and go against it. To be fully effective we also have to recognise and give up any patterns of internalised domination.

At the same time, there is often a lot of confusion about what leadership consists of. Some people are uneasy with the label of leader. Some associate leadership with giving orders or telling people what to do. Many people do not think of themselves as leaders or potential leaders. And many do not see the link between leadership and liberation. So let's take a look at what leadership is really all about.

The Role of a Leader

At workshops, I sometimes ask people what they think is the role of a leader. They suggest that a leader should motivate, give direction, empower people, inspire people, and so on. So the responses are talking about the outcomes that a leader should bring about. That raises the question of what it is leaders have to do to achieve those outcomes. There is something more basic that is at the heart of leadership than these particular outcomes.

A different way of coming at this is to ask people to think about others who made a difference to them in their lives, people who stand out in a special way because of the positive effect they had on them. I ask them, in particular, to list the qualities of these people who came to mind. Common qualities that are highlighted include caring, empathic, accepting, affirming, empowering, supportive, enabling, and so on. Here again, when we examine these lists, it becomes clear that something more basic underlies these qualities. They have something in common with each other.

So what are these underlying factors that allow people to make a difference to the lives of others? It turns out that there is a very simple process or role that underpins all effective leadership. In short, the key role of a leader is to *think* about people. More precisely, the role of a leader is to think about people and the situation facing them. What makes someone a good leader is their ability to think clearly about the people around them. Before they can achieve the outcomes mentioned above, the leader has to think about people and the situation they face. Before they can make a difference to people, they have to think about what's happening to them or about their needs. Before we talk about what leaders do, therefore, let's focus on what it means to think about people.

Thinking About People and the Situation Facing Them

What makes someone effective as a leader is their ability to think clearly or think well in any situation. In a crisis, for example, a leader is someone who can stay thinking when others get confused or get lost in their feelings. Having a leader who can keep thinking in such situations makes a huge difference. When people can tell that someone's mind is working, they stay relaxed and think with the person. On the other hand, in a critical situation, when it looks like those in leadership roles can't think clearly, people's painful feelings come to the surface and start to take over. They start to get lost in their own feelings of fear, confusion, frustration, isolation, and so on. We could see examples of this in the way the Catholic Church handled the revelations of child sexual abuse. It was clear that the leaders of the church were unable to think clearly about this and unable to respond in ways that effectively addressed the needs of those affected. This inability to think clearly created a leadership vacuum and led to many mistakes in the handling of the abuse crisis.

Strengths and Potential

Thinking clearly or well about people involves different elements. To begin with, it includes being able to notice people's strengths. A good leader is tuned in to the talents, abilities and positive qualities of the people around them. This is not just a superficial appreciation of people's strengths or a selective appreciation of some people's strengths. A good leader is all the time noticing any signs of positive qualities, including, and maybe especially, those qualities that the people themselves or other people underestimate.

As well as spotting people's strengths, someone who is leading well also thinks about their potential. They pay attention to the hidden talents or the underdeveloped talents. They try to see what's possible for this person if they got the support, the appreciation or the assistance that would draw out and build on their strengths.

In addition, a good leader doesn't only think about the strengths and potential of individuals. They also think of the strengths and potential of the whole group or the whole community. They have a focus on what we together could accomplish and what needs to happen to reach this potential.

Putting a focus on thinking about potential implies another important aspect of a leader's thinking. Effective leaders tend to think long-term; they don't just think about the current situation. They also think about where things are heading and what's possible in the future. So part of thinking about people's potential is being able to hold out a vision for the future.

Struggles

Leaders don't only think about positive strengths and potential. They also try to think about where people struggle. What are the challenges and difficulties facing people in their lives, their relationships, and within themselves? If we are to make a difference to people, it's not enough to see their strengths and potential. We also need to get a picture of the feelings and external difficulties that hold them back. We think about their struggles but not in a critical way. We want to understand these struggles so we can be a resource for them in tackling them.

As with strengths and potential, we think about the struggles both of the individual and the whole group. We ask ourselves where it gets hard for this person and where it gets hard for this group.

If we think about people who have stood out as great leaders, a key part of what they offered was a clear picture of where people struggled. They were able to name the struggle, and their clarity about this along with their vision about what was possible is what made them effective and inspiring.

Leaders don't just think about people in a vacuum. Part of thinking clearly about people is being able to think about their social identity or about the social context in which they live and work. It means being able to apply what we know about the operation of oppression to understanding their struggles. Making a difference as a leader involves being able to see how people have internalised their oppression and how this affects how they think, feel and act. It also involves being able to see how people have internalised domination and how this affects how they think, feel and act. And it means being able to see how these different effects have an impact on relationships between people with the same social identity and between people of different social identities. In this way, effective leaders see beyond individual 'personalities' and recognise how social identities are central to making sense of what we see happening around us.

Three Questions

In a simple way, the thinking that a leader does can be summed up with three questions that, in one way or another, they are constantly trying to answer. Whether it is in relation to an individual or the whole group, the leader is asking, *What's going on here?* As they get clarity about that, they also ask, *What needs to happen here?* And, finally, they ask, *What support do people need to make this happen?* Leaders know that finding the answers to these three questions is at the heart of leading well.

So leadership is not really about giving orders or telling people what to do. It's about being able to think. Any one of us can do this.

If we can think about the people and the situation around us, we can be a leader. Many of the roles we play in our lives are actually leadership roles except they don't have that label or we don't think of them in that way. Being a parent, for example, is a key leadership role. Caring for or supporting ill and elderly parents is a leadership role. Teaching is a leadership role. Many of us are already leading without thinking of it in that way.

Listening

There is one difficulty with putting thinking at the core of leadership. The problem is that sometimes we don't have enough information to think clearly or the situation is so complex we aren't able to figure it out. Sometimes we're just not knowledgeable or aware enough to see things clearly. So in order to fill out this picture of what it means to lead, we have to add another piece to the role.

If I am to be effective in thinking clearly about people and the situation facing them, I'm going to have to draw on other people's thinking. There is a principle about leading that says it's not possible for one person to do the thinking *for* everyone else. What is possible is to listen to other people in order to fill in the gaps in our own understanding. We can think *with* people and get a clear picture of what's going on and what needs to happen.

Listening is not a straightforward process. The important information we need in order to be clear about any situation can come in a variety of ways. It helps to understand these. In the middle of their struggles, one particular way that people communicate is at the level of feelings. We may ask people what they think but, quite often, they will simply tell us how they are feeling. However, if we listen well to this we will learn very valuable information. In many situations, the most important information comes in this way. (Of course, feelings will also be communicated non-verbally and we have to pay attention to this as well.) All this means that, if

I want to be effective in leading, I have to be comfortable listening to people's feelings and not get side-tracked into being defensive or arguing with them. I can be even more effective if I actively draw out these feelings. In many ways, I cannot fully understand people's struggles unless I have a clear picture of how these struggles leave them feeling.

Apart from showing us their feelings, another important way that people communicate is by telling us stories or anecdotes about what's happening in their lives. Again, we might ask someone what they think about things but instead of giving us their thinking they tell us a story about what happened to them last week. It may be a story about a crisis they faced or something that frustrated them or about some way that things did not go as they expected or hoped. If we listen well to this story, we will learn a lot about where they struggle.

In both these cases, feelings and stories, if we listen widely to many people, we will begin to see a pattern in what we are hearing. We'll hear the same feelings being expressed by different people or we'll hear similar stories about what's happening for people. What may have been confusing to begin with gradually begins to come together in an overall picture of the situation. Each person we listen to adds a piece to the jigsaw. Individually, they may not have been able to paint a clear picture but, together, the feelings they showed us and the stories they told us allow us to make sense of the situation. The understanding we gain can then be fed back to them as part of pointing a way forward. Someone captured this once when they said that the role of a leader was to reflect back to people in a challenging way the issues that they themselves raised in a confused way.

Not everyone will communicate with feelings and stories. Some people will have very clear thinking to offer. They have a deep understanding of the struggle, and if we listen well, we will learn a huge amount from them. Sometimes important perspectives or pieces of thinking will come from someone other than the named leader. What makes that leader effective is the ability to listen to this other person's good thinking and use it to clarify their own thinking. This will sometimes be the case where the person trying to lead has an oppressor identity. Inevitably, their thinking will not be as clear about the struggle as the thinking of people from the oppressed group. Their effectiveness as a leader depends on being able to learn from and be guided by the thinking of oppressed people.

In this way, listening is a key leadership skill. In practice, most of the important listening takes place casually, informally and spontaneously rather than in formal meetings. It often happens in short snatches, in passing, or while we are engaged in another task with someone. We stop to greet someone, for example, and ask them about their day. In the space of a few minutes we pick up important pieces of information that help clarify our understanding of things. I have often thought that a very useful skill for a leader is the ability to apparently 'waste time' with people, during which they get to listen. One practical skill that aids this is the simple ability to pay good attention and not interrupt when people are showing us their feelings, telling us a story or sharing their thinking.

Building Relationships

Putting an emphasis on listening well leads to another important aspect of leading. The only way I will hear what I need to hear in order to think well is to get close to people. At the heart of all effective leadership is the building of solid one-to-one relationships; the real work of leading is done one-to-one. Meetings, committees and teams are part of making things happen but they are no substitute for building relationships and getting close to people individually. This means we can sometimes assess the quality of our leadership by looking at what's happening in our relationships.

- How well are we connected to people?

- Who do we not have a solid relationship with?

- Is there anyone we have been neglecting?

- Who have we not paid attention to recently?

- Who have we lost touch with?

In the end, we cannot lead people effectively at a distance. We have to get close to those we want to lead.

GOOD LEADERSHIP

We can take these three aspects of the leader's role and use them to define good leadership. From this point of view, good leadership is a process of building close relationships with people, within which we listen well to them, so that we can think clearly about them and the situation facing them.

Notice that, by this definition, *everyone* is a potential leader. It's not something rare or special that only a few people are capable of. Anyone can decide to build relationships, listen and think. Because of the particular hurts we carry and the effects of oppression, some people are in better shape to take on this role at any given moment but we can all make the decision to reach for it. For anyone new to leading and wondering where to begin, it's not that complicated. Start making connections with people and listening to them. If we do that well, the next steps soon become clear.

The important thing here is that deciding to take leadership, particularly around our oppression, is a huge contradiction to our internalised powerlessness. The simple act of deciding to get close to people and listen to them pulls us out of any feelings of being a victim and connects us with our power. It shifts our attention away from how bad we feel and onto how we can be a resource for the people around us.

OTHER PARTS OF THE LEADERSHIP ROLE

In taking these simple but powerful steps towards leading, other parts of the leadership role become clearer. As we listen and come to understand people's struggles, we begin to see a vision of how things could be and we get ideas about how to move towards that vision. This vision is not something pulled out of the air; it's not something that comes from the outside. Vision is intimately connected to the quality of our relationships and our listening. In a simple way, vision is the other side of struggle. Once we understand the struggle, the vision follows.

Based on what we've heard and how it helps shape our understanding of the situation and our vision, we say to people, *How about if we did this?* We propose a way forward. Sometimes this makes good sense and people readily agree with what we propose. At other times, they see flaws in our thinking and we have to listen more before coming up with an alternative. Sometimes our suggestion triggers a better one from someone else in the group. This is all part of leading well. Based on the best thinking available, we propose ways forward and get agreement.

Finally, we take action to address the struggles and challenges we have identified and this highlights one other quality of leading well: decisiveness. Part of thinking well is knowing when it's time to act. There comes a time when we have talked enough and action is necessary. Most of the time, we will get consensus or a working agreement on what steps to take. Occasionally, there won't be consensus. If the issue is not a critical or urgent one, we can decide to keep listening and thinking together until consensus emerges. If the issue *is* critical or urgent, however, in the absence of consensus the leader may say, *Having listened to everyone, here's what I think we should do.* In most cases, if people feel they have been listened to well, they will recognise the need for action and agree to what the leader proposes, even if it is not what they personally would prefer. The critical factor is that they feel they have been listened to.

What we have to understand is that prolonged indecision can have hugely negative effects on a group. Where this happens, people's worst qualities tend to come to the surface. They become frustrated, angry, discouraged, impatient, divisive or any of a range of other negative reactions and with these the group begins to fall apart. Thinking well means recognising when this point has been reached and acting decisively.

SOCIAL CHANGE

Deciding to take leadership of any kind is a powerful way to weaken the hold of internalised oppression and domination. Taking leadership specifically to bring about social change is even more powerful. Not only do we take steps to heal the hurts we personally have experienced and to contradict our own internalised oppression, we also decide to change the social conditions that give rise to oppression in the first place. We cannot ultimately be free of hurt as long as oppression continues, so, in its fullest sense, true leadership is leadership for liberation.

So what does liberation leadership involve? Using what we saw earlier as the different elements of leadership, liberation leadership consists of:

• building relationships with other oppressed people that cut across any isolation or divisiveness,

• listening to their experiences of oppression and creating safety for them to discharge the hurts they have endured,

- learning from them about the oppression and its effects,

- creating a vision of what liberation would look like,

- building a community of people who are committed to change,

- finding opportunities to raise awareness among other people and win allies,

- assisting people to organise and supporting them to take action to bring about change.

There is no blueprint for social change. It begins with a simple decision to make a difference and work for change. At this point we don't know how we will do it, but, as the vision becomes clearer, we gradually complete the steps that are necessary to achieve our goal. Making that initial decision has the capacity to transform our lives.

ONE MAJOR CHALLENGE

Oppressive systems are not rational. They rest on a range of painful emotions including greed and fear. Over time and with the development of ever more sophisticated technology, they have the capacity to become increasingly destructive. If we look at the world around us, we see a system that is hugely unstable and practically unworkable for large numbers of people. There are many signs of this:

- The gap between rich and poor globally is increasing dramatically and we have seen a huge transfer of wealth from the bottom to the top.

- There is a global rise in unemployment and an increasing proportion of low-paid, zero-hour, precarious jobs.

- We see growing religious fundamentalism and extremism leading to violence and counter-violence.

• Conflicts between different social groupings are increasing, with right-wing appeals to racism and xenophobia.

• There are huge and growing numbers of displaced people and refugees globally.

• There is continuing destructive exploitation of the environment.

• There is growing tension between major world powers.

• The threat of nuclear destruction, which we thought had receded in the aftermath of the cold war, is once more a dangerous reality.

In addition to these sources of instability, we have an economic system that goes from periods of boom to bust. The system tends to lurch from one crisis to another, each time managing to recover, at least for those on top, before the cycle repeats itself once again. In the normal run of events, it could presumably continue in this way indefinitely. However, these times are not normal. There is one major challenge facing us for which we are extremely unprepared: global warming. When we add the predictions about global warming to the mix of other sources of instability, we can see that we are rapidly approaching a critical point in human history. The global economic system is based on continuing growth, exploitation of the environment and profit. Such a system is incompatible with a sustainable environment and habitable planet. As a point of no return rapidly approaches and as governments fail to take the necessary steps to prevent a catastrophic rise in temperature, the system will become increasingly unstable and unworkable, with the potential for huge destruction. We got a small glimpse of what that might mean with the crash of 2008. More and more experts are now saying it is not a question of *if* but of *when* the next big crash comes. It is quite plausible to suggest that we shall see the complete collapse of the current global economic system within the lifetimes of people alive today, particularly younger people. We know from history that periods of collapse have the potential to be very destructive, so part of the challenge we face is to manage the collapse to avoid widespread destruction and enable a transition to a more rational and sustainable system.

More than ever, the need for fundamental social and systemic change is vital. This means that liberation leadership has a key role to play in creating a sustainable, egalitarian, non-destructive and just social system. At this stage in our history, liberation leadership is not just about eliminating oppression, it is about ensuring a sustainable future for all the people on the planet. Deciding to end oppression is a hugely empowering and liberating step to take. Deciding to see that we have a habitable planet to live on can propel us way beyond any confusion about our own struggles or any doubts about our own inherent humanity. In one way, looking at the prospects ahead could increase our sense of hopelessness. Actually, however, this challenge we face presents us with huge opportunities to create a better world and huge opportunities to reclaim and experience our true power.

The answers to the problems we will face are unlikely to come from oppressor groups with a vested interest in the maintenance of their privileged positions. Individuals from these groups may help to make important contributions but, overall, these groups will not be the source of the answers we need. More and more, the necessary leadership will come from within oppressed groups. Their position gives them a more realistic perspective on the world that is much more likely to inform creative solutions. Four groups in particular come to mind as having a key role to play in shaping the world to come: women, young people, indigenous people and people of colour. There is tremendous power, creativity, understanding, passion and intelligence, among many other important qualities, within these groups that give them the potential to make an enormous difference. For people from these groups and other oppressed groups, the challenges facing us offer the possibility of big lives and big leadership organised around liberation and changing the world rather than the narrow lives and limited leadership currently on offer. For those of us from oppressor groups, the challenge is to support and back the leadership of people from groups such as these, listen to their thinking and follow their lead, and, in doing this, we also get to have big lives and big leadership of a very different kind to what we presently have.

CONCLUSION

A key part of taking charge of our struggles is deciding to take leadership. In many ways, leadership is a simple process. It is not a position we occupy, it is something we do. At its core, it involves building relationships with the people around us, listening to them and thinking about what we see and hear. Making a decision to change the world around us is even more powerful.

Seeing the close link between our social identities, our experience of oppression and our personal struggles changes the way we think about ourselves and the world around us. It allows us to move away from self-doubt, self-blame, shame and hopelessness and turn our struggles into sources of growth and empowerment. As we go against our internalised oppression and domination, reconnect with our inherent human qualities, and reclaim our power by taking leadership, we build a completely different relationship with ourselves and with the people in our lives. By deciding to make a difference to the world around us and help create a viable and sustainable future based on justice, respect, care of the environment, and equality, we leave behind any traces of being victims and take on a life that is big, exciting and enriching. In the end, understanding the true origins of our struggles liberates and transforms us.

Questions

1. In considering leadership as a process of thinking, listening and building relationships, what are your strengths as a leader?

2. What would you do differently that would make you an even more effective leader?

3. What are the challenges or struggles facing people around you and what support do they need?

GLOSSARY

Discharge
The release of feelings through crying, laughing, shaking, angry noises, hot or cold perspiration, or yawning. Discharge is often part of the healing process.

Healing
The process of recovering from our hurts through the release of painful feelings and the reclaiming of our connection to our inherent human characteristics.

Identity
The various social groups we belong to by birth, that we become part of as we grow up, or that others perceive us to belong to. The salient identities are the ones that have played a key role in shaping how we think, feel and behave and how we view ourselves.

Inherent characteristics
The characteristics that are true of us as humans. These are universally true of all people and are considered to be permanent in spite of any hurts or disconnection from them that we acquire.

Internalised domination
The patterns of behaviour, thinking and feeling that we internalise as a result of our experiences of having power and privilege.

Internalised oppression
The patterns of behaviour, thinking and feeling that we accept and absorb and then internalise as a result of our experiences of being oppressed.

Leadership
The action of leading a group or organisation, or being regarded as the person who does so. The process of building relationships within which we listen to people so that we can think about them, and the actions we take based on this.

Oppressed identities

The groups we belong to that experience oppression and our identification with these groups.

Oppression

The systematic, one-way mistreatment of the members of one group by those of another group or by society as a whole.

Oppressor identities

The groups we belong to that are the agents of the oppression of other groups in society.

OTHER RESOURCES

This information about services and supports, across public and voluntary sectors, has been compiled for readers, with particular emphasis on resources relevant to this book. However, the directory cannot be, nor does it claim to be, comprehensive, and further information about regional and local services may be obtained through their websites or national branch offices.

In providing this list no personal recommendation with regard to the services listed is made or implied by the author or by the publishers. While every effort has been made to ensure that the information given is accurate and up-to-date, no responsibility can be taken in the event of errors.

Additionally, it is always recommended that in any situation of concern people seek professional advice, and in relation to health or mental health that they consult their local general practitioner or health authority.

Age Action Ireland: **www.ageaction.ie**
(Information and support for older people)

Anti-Bullying Centre: **www.antibullyingcentre.ie**
(Help and advice on bullying)

Aware: **www.aware.ie**
(Support and information on anxiety and depression)

Barnardos: **www.barnardos.ie**
(Support for children, young people and families in need)

Bodywhys: **www.bodywhys.ie**
(The Eating Disorders Association of Ireland)

Bullying at Work:
www.hsa.ie/eng/Workplace_Health/Bullying_at_Work
(Support for those affected by bulling at work)

Carers Association: **www.carersireland.com**
(Advice and information for carers)

Critical Voices Network: **www.cvni.ie/index.php**
(Information and advice on mental health issues)

Disability Federation of Ireland: **www.disability-federation.ie**
(Support and information for people with a disability)

European Network Against Racism: **www.enar-eu.org**
(Advice and information on racism)

Family Therapy Association of Ireland: **www.familytherapyireland.com**
(Information on therapy for individuals, couples and families)

Focus Ireland: **www.focusireland.ie**
(Support and information for people affected by homelessness)

Health Service Executive: **www.hse.ie/eng/services/list**
(Supports provided by the national health service)

Irish Council for Psychotherapy: **www.psychotherapycouncil.ie**
(Information on psychotherapy services in Ireland)

Irish Feminist Network: **www.irishfeministnetwork.org**
(Information on all aspects of gender equality)

Irish Refugee Council: **www.irishrefugeecouncil.ie**
(Advice and support for refugees in Ireland)

Irish Traveller Movement: **www.itmtrav.ie**
(Support and information for members of the Traveller community)

Jigsaw: **www.jigsaw.ie**
(The National Centre for Youth Mental Health)

Men's Development Network: **www.mens-network.net**
(Working with men towards achieving beneficial change)

Mental Health Ireland: **www.mentalhealthireland.ie**
(Promotion of positive mental health in Ireland)

National LGBT Federation: **www.nxf.ie**
(Information and advice for the LGBT community)

National Women's Council: **www.nwci.ie**
(Working towards equality for women)

Pavee Point Traveller and Roma Centre: **www.paveepoint.ie**
(Support and information for members of the Traveller and Roma
communities)

Pieta House: **www.pieta.ie**
(Advice and support for people affected by suicide)

Psychological Society of Ireland: **www.psychologicalsociety.ie**
(Professional body for psychology and psychologists in the Republic
of Ireland)

Rape Crisis Centres: **www.rcni.ie**
(Information and support for victims of sexual violence)

Samaritans: **www.samaritans.org/ireland**
(Confidential 24-hour support service for people who are depressed,
suicidal or in need)

Victim Support: **www.crimevictimshelpline.ie**
(Support and information for people affected by crime)

Women's Aid: **www.womensaid.ie**
(Support for women and children affected by domestic abuse)

OTHER READING

The ideas laid out in this book are based on many years of experience leading workshops in different parts of the world on the theme of leadership and liberation, working with a wide range of identity groups, working through the effects of my own experiences as an oppressed person and an oppressor, and reading the works of particular authors who have dealt with many of these same issues in their own lives. If you would like to explore this topic further, below are some publications that deal with themes from this book.

Adam, B.D., *The Survival of Domination: Inferiorization and everyday life* (New York: Elsevier North-Holland, 1978)

Allport, G., *The Nature of Prejudice* (25th anniversary edn) (Reading, MA: Addison-Wesley, 1979)

Barnes, B., *The Nature of Power* (Cambridge: Polity, 1988)

Barnett, P.E., 'Discussions across Difference: Addressing the affective dimensions of teaching diverse students about diversity', *Teaching in Higher Education*, vol. 16, no. 6, 2011, pp. 669–79

Boakye, J., *Black, Listed: Black British culture explored* (London: Dialogue Books, 2019)

Brown, C. and Mazza, G., *Leading Diverse Communities: A how-to guide for moving from healing into action* (San Francisco: Jossey-Bass, 2005)

Burnham, J., Alvis Palma, D. and Whitehouse, L., 'Learning as a Context for Differences and Differences as a Context for Learning', *Journal of Family Therapy*, vol. 30, no. 4, 2008, pp. 529–42

Burnham, J., 'Developments in Social GGRRAAACCEEESSS: Visible-invisible, voiced-unvoiced', in I. Krause (ed.), *Cultural Reflexivity* (London: Karnac Books, 2013)

David, E.J.R. (ed.), *Internalized Oppression: The psychology of marginalized groups* (New York: Springer Publishing, 2014)

Divac, A. and Heaphy, G., 'Space for GRRAACCES: Training for cultural competence in supervision', *Journal of Family Therapy*, vol. 27, 2005, pp. 280–4

Fanon, F., *Decolonizing Madness: The psychiatric writings of Frantz Fanon* (London: Palgrave Macmillan, 2019)

Foucault, M., *Power/Knowledge: Selected interviews and other writings, 1972–1977* (New York: Vintage, 1980)

Franklin, A., Fox, H. and Carey, M., *An Invitation to Narrative Practitioners to Address Privilege and Dominance* (2004), https://dulwichcentre.com.au/a-continuing-invitation-to-narrative-practitioners-to-address-privilege-and-dominance [accessed 29 May 2019]

Freire, P., *Pedagogy of the Oppressed* (Harmondsworth: Penguin, 1972)

Golder, B., *Re-reading Foucault: On law, power and rights* (London: Routledge, 2013)

Harré, R., *Personal Being* (Cambridge, MA: Harvard University Press, 1984)

Harré, R., Clarke, D. and De Carlo, N., *Motives and Mechanisms: An introduction to the psychology of action* (London: Methuen, 1985)

Harré, R., 'Language Games and the Texts of Identity', in J. Shotter and K.J. Gergen (eds), *Texts of Identity* (London: Sage Publications, 1989)

Harter, S., *The Construction of the Self: Developmental and sociocultural foundations* (New York: Guilford Press, 2012)

Jackins, H., *The Human Side of Human Beings* (Seattle: Rational Island, 1978)

Jones, C. and Porter, R., *Reassessing Foucault: Power, medicine and the body* (London: Routledge, 1994)

Kanter, R.M., *Men and Women of the Corporation* (New York: Basic Books, 1993)

Mac Gréil, M., *Prejudice in Ireland Revisited* (Maynooth: Survey and Research Unit, St Patrick's College, 1996)

Mason, B. and Sawyerr, A. (eds), *Exploring the Unsaid: Creativity, risks, and dilemmas in working cross-culturally* (London: Karnac Books, 2002)

Mead, G.H., *Mind, Self, and Society from the Standpoint of a Social Behaviorist*, edited by C.W. Morris (Chicago: University of Chicago Press, 1967)

Memmi, A., *The Colonizer and the Colonized* (London: Earthscan, 1990)

Moane, G., *Gender and Colonialism: A psychological analysis of oppression* (Houndmills: Palgrave Macmillan, 2011)

Mullaly, B., *Challenging Oppression: A critical social work approach* (Don Mills, ON: Oxford University Press, 2002)

Rost, J., *Leadership for the Twenty-First Century* (Westport, CT: Praeger, 1993)

Ruth, S., 'Middle-Class Activists and Social Change', *Studies*, vol. 94, no. 372, 2005, pp. 51–60

Ruth, S., 'Responding to Abuse: Culture, leadership and change', in John Littleton and Eamon Maher (eds), *The Dublin/Murphy Report: A watershed for Irish Catholicism* (Dublin: Columba Press, 2010), pp. 102–12

Ruth, S., *Leadership and Liberation: A psychological approach* (Hove: Routledge, 2012)

Shotter, J., 'Social Accountability and Self Specification', in K. Gergen and K. Davis (eds), *Social Construction of the Person* (New York: Springer Publishing, 1985)

Shotter, J. and Gergen, K.J. (eds), *Texts of Identity* (London: Sage Publications, 1989)

Shotter, J., *Conversational Realities: Constructing life through language* (London: Sage Publications, 1993)

Smail, D., *Illusion and Reality: The meaning of anxiety* (London: Karnac Books, 1984)

Totsuka, Y., 'Which Aspects of Social GGRRAAACCEEESSS Grab You Most?' The social GGRRAAACCEEESSS exercise for a supervision group to promote therapists' self-reflexivity', *Journal of Family Therapy*, vol. 36, S1, 2014

INDEX

acceptance, 104
accidents, 17–18, 41
addictions, 45, 52
adoption, 9, 35
alcohol, 45, 52
allies, 39–40, 81, 84–5, 98
anger, 75, 77–8, 90–97, 102
arrogance, 25, 26, 37, 62, 101
assimilation, 45, 52, 90
assumptions, 23, 54
austerity measures, 32
automatic responses, 69–71
awareness, 36–7, 96, 104, 122
awkwardness, 23

basic cultural competence, 37
begrudgery, 51
Behan, Brendan, 48
boom and bust economy, 123
bribes, 55–6

charismatic leaders, 91
civil rights movement, 71
claiming identity, 13–14
class, 9, 10–11, 38–9, 55–60
class oppression, 38–9
climate change, 123
condescension, 25, 26
conditioning, 14, 56, 60, 63–4,
    98, 104
conflict management, 70
contagion, 17–18, 41
consciousness-raising, 34
criminality, 52, 95
crying, 73, 74–5
cultural blindness, 35–6
cultural competency, 34–8, 101
cultural destructiveness, 35
cultural incapacity, 35

cultural narrowing, 49–50
cultural pre-competence, 36
cultural proficiency, 37

debt, 32
decisiveness, 120–21
defiance, 52, 93, 102
denial, 59–60, 102
devaluation, 62
discharge of feelings, 73–9, 97
disconnection, 57
discrimination, 25, 35
discussion, 79–80
displaced violence, 94
divisiveness, 48–9, 93
drugs, 45, 52

Easter Rising, 90
economic instability, 123–4
economic oppression, 31, 32
education, 91
embarrassment, 76–7
empowerment, 96–7
entitlement, 54, 62, 90, 94, 101–2
environment, 123
ethnic cleansing, 35
exclusion, 25, 49–50

fear, 35, 56, 75–6, 94
flexible responses, 68–9

gambling, 52
Gandhi, Mahatma, 91
gender, 8, 9, 10–11, 36, 55–60, 71–2,
    75, 80–81, 99, 102
genocide, 32, 35
global warming, 123
grief, 74–5
guilt, 103–4

harassment, 25
healing process
    discharge of feelings, 73–9
    and listening, 71–3, 79–82,
        83–5, 97
    overcoming internalised
        domination, 82–5
    support groups, 79–82
    telling stories, 71–3
health, 45
homophobia, 9, 56
honesty, 82–5
hopelessness, 47, 94–5, 101, 124
humanity, 14–17, 57, 60–61, 100,
    105, 108–9
hurt
    effects of, 16–17, 22, 68–71, 108
    and internalised domination, 60–61
    recovery from, 18, 71–85
    sources of, 17–18

immigrants, 49
imprisonment, 32
incentives, 55–6
incitement to hatred, 33, 49, 94, 123
indigenous peoples, 32, 35, 52, 124
inequalities, 10, 33, 38, 58, 122
inherent characteristics, 14–17, 22,
    108–9
insensitive language, 25, 26
internalised domination
    and humanity, 60–61, 105
    internalisation process, 54–5
    and the liberation process, 94, 100,
        104–5
    mechanisms encouraging oppressor
        roles, 55–60
    overcoming, 82–5
    patterns of domination, 61–4
    unavoidable nature of, 63–4
internalised oppression
    acting out of, 29

characteristics of, 46–54
contradicting of, 109–10
examples of, 45
internalisation process, 28–9
as a layer of oppression, 31, 34
and the liberation process, 92–3, 96,
    99, 100

judgement, distortion of, 69

King, Martin Luther, 50, 91

labels, 9, 14, 92
land appropriation, 35
language suppression, 35, 52, 90
laughter, 76–7, 78
leadership
    attacking of leaders, 50–51, 93
    challenges to overcome, 122–5
    charismatic leaders, 91
    and decisiveness, 120–21
    and effecting social change, 121–2
    good leadership, 119–20
    and listening, 116–18, 120–21
    meaning of leadership, 111–12
    by members of oppressed groups,
        104, 124–5
    and recognising strengths and
        potential, 113–14
    and recognising struggles, 114–15
    and relationship-building, 118–19,
        121
    role of a leader, 112–19
    and thinking about people, 112–13
    and vision, 120, 122
liberation process
    angry phase, 90–97
    and empowerment, 96–7
    independent phase, 97–9
    and internalised domination, 94,
        100, 104–5

and internalised oppression, 92–3, 96, 99, 100
and leadership, 121–2, 124
liberated phase, 100–101
oppressed phase, 88–90
oppressor liberation, 101–5
stages of liberation, 88–101
and violence, 93–7
light anger, 78
listening
and cultural competency, 37
and the healing process, 71–3, 79–82, 83–5, 97
and leadership, 116–18, 120–21
and overcoming internalised domination, 83–5
and support groups, 79–82
low expectations, 25, 26, 35, 45
low pay, 32, 122
low self-esteem, 46–7

Mandela, Nelson, 91
manipulativeness, 45, 52
mass media, 33, 59, 91, 96
#me too movement, 59
memories, 83
mental health system, 33, 68
micro-assaults, 26
misinformation, 58–9, 62
mistreatment, 24–7, 30, 63, 88–9
mistrust of own thinking, 51
monopolisation, 63, 80
Muslims, 49, 94

negative messages, 27, 29, 109–10
negative self-image, 27–8
non-violent action, 96–7
nuclear threat, 123

offensive jokes, 25–6
oppressed identities, 10–13, 22–4

oppression
class oppression, 38–9
and cultural competency, 34–8
defining oppression, 30–31
economic oppression, 31, 32
interlinked nature of oppressions, 53, 96, 100–101
internalised oppression see internalised oppression
levels of oppression, 31–4
liberation from, 88–105
oppressed and oppressor identities, 10–13
oppressed groups, 22–4
oppression process, 22–9
origins of, 40–41
overt vs. subtle oppression, 25–7, 64, 102
physical oppression, 31, 32
psychological oppression, 31, 32–3
as source of hurt, 18, 22
of young people, 68, 101
oppressor identities, 10–13
oppressor liberation, 101–5
oppressor roles, adoption of, 53, 55–60, 94
outrage, 77–8
overt oppression, 25–7, 64, 102

Parks, Rosa, 90–91
paternalism, 35, 101–2
personality, 7–8, 48, 115
pharmaceutical industry, 33
physical oppression, 31, 32
physical tension, 78–9
political independence, 95–6
politicians, 33
populism, 94
potential, 113–14
poverty, 32, 40
poverty insertion programmes, 40

power, 30, 65, 72, 94, 96–7, 110–11
powerlessness, 47–8, 89, 94–5,
    119–20
precarious work, 32, 122
prejudice, 9, 22–3, 37, 39, 82–3, 94,
    104
pride, 92–3, 97, 102, 104, 110
privilege, 54, 62, 90, 101–2
psychological oppression, 31, 32–3

race, 10–11, 58, 60, 63–4, 72
racketeering, 52, 95
rape, 32
recovery *see* healing process
refugees, 49, 94, 123
relationship-building, 118–19, 121
religion suppression, 35, 90
religious fundamentalism, 122
rigid niceness, 25, 26

safety, 72, 73, 74, 76, 78, 80, 81, 82–5
salient identities, 8–10
sanctions, 56–7
segregation, 32, 35
self-destructive behaviours, 45, 52
self-esteem, 46–7, 72, 97
self-image, 27–8
separation, 57–8, 62
sexual abuse, 32, 36, 60, 63
sexual orientation, 8–9, 10–11, 56,
    58, 72
shaking, 76
Sinn Féin, 96
slavery, 41
social change, 121–2
social identity
    claiming identity, 13–14
    explaining concept of, 7–8
    and feelings, 11–13
    oppressed and oppressor identities,
        10–13
    salient identities, 8–10

social media, 99
stereotypes, 9, 22, 33, 35, 58–9, 62
stories, 8, 13–14, 71–3, 79–82, 117
strengths, 113–14
struggles
    explaining concept of, 7
    and leadership, 114–15
    taking charge of, 108–25
subtle oppression, 25–7, 64, 102
superiority, 26, 35, 39, 54, 62, 90, 94,
    101–2
support groups, 79–82
survival strategies, 51–4
sweating, 76, 77

thinking
    and leadership, 112–13, 115–16
    about people, 112–13
    and discharge of feelings, 73, 76, 77
    effects of hurt upon, 68–70
threats, 56–7
tokenism, 36, 104
trauma, 15, 16
Travellers, 29, 52, 58
triggering events, 90–91
unemployment, 32, 122

verbal abuse, 25
violence, 25, 32, 63, 93–7, 102, 122
vision, 120, 122

Watson, Lilla, 38
women's movement, 71–2, 99
working the system, 45, 52

yawning, 78–9
young people, 68, 74–5, 101, 124

zero-hour contracts, 32, 122